The Last Fancy Dan

THE DUNCAN McKENZIE STORY

The Last Fancy Dan

THE DUNCAN McKENZIE STORY

Duncan McKenzie with David Saffer

VERTICAL EDITIONS

www.verticaleditions.com

First published in the United Kingdom in 2009 by
Vertical Editions, Unit 4a, Snaygill Industrial Estate,
Skipton, North Yorkshire BD23 2QR

www.verticaleditions.com

A CIP catalogue record for this book is available
from the British Library

'The Magic of McKenzie' © Paul Cookson, Poet in
Residence at the National Football Museum
www.paulcooksonpoet.co.uk

ISBN 978-1-904091-36-3

Cover design and typeset by HBA, York

Printed and bound by The MPG Books Group,
Bodmin

CONTENTS

ACKNOWLEDGEMENTS

I'd like to thank Karl Waddicor at Vertical Editions for agreeing to publish Duncan's autobiography, editor Diane Evans, and my good friend Phil Goldstone for allowing me open access to his Aladdin's cave of statistical football books. Being able to help Duncan chronicle his career on and off the park has been a privilege and fun all the way.

David Saffer

THE MAGIC OF McKENZIE
(For Duncan McKenzie)

You wore your sleeves long
Bunched in your hands
Languid, almost lazy
The magic of McKenzie

Out of the ordinary
Sublimely talented
Fleet of feet
The magic of McKenzie

Born entertainer
Extravagant showman
Indulgent yet unmissable
The magic of McKenzie

We all knew
That you could leap
Over a Mini Cooper
The magic of McKenzie

Thrower of a golf ball
The length of a football pitch
Individual and maverick
The magic of McKenzie

More than a fairground attraction
More than a circus sideshow
We flattered, you deceived and we believed
In the magic of McKenzie

Paul Cookson
Poet in Residence at The National Football Museum

INTRODUCTION

Duncan McKenzie demonstrated the artistry of football alongside other notable maverick footballers Stan Bowles, Frank Worthington, Rodney Marsh, Tony Currie, Charlie George and Alan Hudson in an era when pitches were often ankle deep in mud, waterlogged or frozen. And tough nut defenders loved nothing more than taking out a player that threatened to waltz through a defence or take the mickey with improvised skill they could only dream of possessing.

McKenzie was the star player at Nottingham Forest when he arrived at Leeds United in the summer of 1974 for a record transfer fee. The first signing for new boss Brian Clough, Cloughie soon left the club following his infamous 44-day stay but his legacy was a footballer who would become a cult hero during a two-year stint at the club.

McKenzie was a genius on the ball but he was also something of an enigma because you never quite knew what this magician of a player would do as the ball came to him. Would the Leeds striker trap the ball in an instant, nutmeg an opponent, go on a mazy run or strike for goal with aplomb? Playing off the cuff, McKenzie wooed the Elland Road faithful and there was an air of anticipation whenever the ball made its way in his direction. And naturally his cult hero status was replicated during future spells at Anderlecht, Everton, Chelsea, Blackburn Rovers and Stateside with Tulsa Roughnecks and Chicago Sting.

But this talented footballer was not just an entertainer on the pitch. Former colleagues at Forest lost many a bet with Duncan's hurdling ability over a training gate while Leeds teammates gasped as he cleared a Mini for fun and lost bets galore with his golf ball throwing ability. For good measure Duncan made his mark at the annual Christmas Panto. On Merseyside, Evertonians tuned in to hear him as a consummate radio presenter on *Mac 'n' Tosh* while businessmen laughed along to his patter at corporate events. And since hanging up his boots, this quite extraordinary character has carved out a second career as one of the most popular after-dinner speakers on the circuit up and down the country.

This charismatic personality may have missed out on picking up major honours and failed to make the England XI despite being in numerous squads, but ask football supporters of the era which opposing players were danger men and entertained them for good measure and the name McKenzie is up there with the best. And rightly so because make no mistake, Duncan McKenzie made his mark on the game during his career.

Come rain or shine, rock hard surface or quagmire pitch, McKenzie gave the likes of hatchet men Ron 'Chopper' Harris, Norman 'Bites Yer Legs' Hunter and Tommy Smith a run for their money. And when it came to putting the ball in the net, he delivered time and time again because, just as thousands of supporters sang from the terraces up and down the country. . . Duncan McKenzie was magic.

Enjoy the reminiscences.

David Saffer, 2009

1

FOOTBALL DREAMS

During my pomp as a professional footballer in the seventies I was dubbed a luxury player, a maverick and a nearly-man at Nottingham Forest, Leeds United, Anderlecht, Everton, Chelsea and Blackburn Rovers, not to forget a spell in the American national soccer league with Tulsa Roughnecks and Chicago Sting and finally a brief sojourn in Hong Kong. I heard all the comments—McKenzie nearly played for England, nearly won major honours and nearly had a glorious career. So-called football experts loved or loathed me, opponents admired or berated me and teammates felt inspired or exasperated in equal measure. Supporters dubbed me an entertainer and I'm eternally grateful for that accolade because I played the game off the cuff, on the edge and with a smile.

From entertaining football skills on the park I've been privileged to transfer my entertainment skills onto the after-dinner circuit, regaling audiences with anecdotal tales and opinions surrounding such footballing legends, celebrity fanatics and modern day heroes as George Best, Pele, Maradona, Bobby Moore, Billy Bremner, Bobby Charlton, Kevin Keegan, Brian Clough, Bill Shankly, Frank Worthington, Stan Bowles, Sir Norman Wisdom, Jimmy Tarbuck, David Beckham, Wayne

Rooney and Steven Gerrard. Whether bamboozling defenders on a football field, jumping over Minis to make a few bob, hosting football chat shows on radio or making 'em laugh at a sportsman's dinner, my football journey continues to be fun. From nutmegs to magical goals, cup final despair, international heartache, US razzmatazz and stand-up comedy, it's been a helter-skelter trek.

Like thousands of starry-eyed kids knocking a football about with mates in the street or park, I had dreams of becoming a professional footballer when I grew up in my hometown of Grimsby. And when my hopes were realised, nobody could stop me playing the game my way and eventually 'my way' gained acceptance from previous doubters.

Former Nottingham Forest teammate Sammy Chapman would say to me, 'McKenzie, you're a frustrating bugger but anyone who scores 20 goals a season can do what he wants.' At Leeds United, I scored twice in a 2–0 win against Arsenal at Elland Road, but that did not stop Leeds' iconic midfielder Johnny Giles ticking me off when I went on a solo run looking for a hat-trick with a teammate better placed. Giles was a winner and personal glory went out of the window until the final whistle but he was the first to give me a nod of approval and slap on the back for being the match winner. Playing for Anderlecht, where laid-back football was the norm, Dutch star Robbie Rensenbrink said I was more an entertainer than footballer and Arie Haan believed my style was more continental than British. Both descriptions delighted me. Finally, at Everton, Bruce Rioch, a gifted midfield schemer, told me after we'd finished playing that he envied the free spirit with which I played the game because of the reaction I got from Evertonians.

During my career I played under a plethora of managers including Johnny Carey, Bill Anderson, Matt Gillies, Dave Mackay, Allan Brown, Tom Eggleston, Danny Williams, Brian

Clough, Jimmy Armfield, Raymond Goethals, Billy Bingham and Gordon Lee. My style was not for all of them but I had my fans. Forest boss Dave Mackay changed the direction of my career by encouraging me to try my repertoire of flicks and tricks. Brian ('Cloughie' as he was affectionately known in the game) made me his first signing at Leeds United. Sadly, we barely had a chance to work together during his infamous 44-day spell at Elland Road but there was time for his words of wisdom to motivate me throughout my career.

Of all these bosses though, Mansfield Town manager Danny Williams, not a household name by any means, was first to spot and really boost my confidence when things were not going well in my early days as a pro at Forest. During a second loan spell, Danny was standing on the sidelines in his galoshes for my first training session, as the training ground was ankle deep in mud. In his thick Yorkshire accent, Danny yelled, 'Thee lad . . . play out wide on't left!' I made no impression. Danny yelled, 'All reet then lad . . . play out on't right!' I did and failed to deliver. Danny was determined. He yelled, 'Reet lad . . . thee go in't middle and play alongside Wiggy!' Frank Wignall was a former Everton star coming to the end of his career. I moved alongside Wiggy but still struggled. Danny was frustrated but did not need to worry. A Mansfield lad had a word and Danny suddenly gave me a free role. Danny yelled, 'Reet lad . . . do t'own thing. Let's see what thee can do!'

I thought, 'Okay!' Picking the ball up on halfway, I went on a solo run, dummied past a couple of opponents and chipped the keeper for a goal. Danny yelled, 'Reet lads . . . that'll do, training's over!' My confidence was back and it paid off with goals galore.

In the late eighties and early nineties there was a cult football programme called *Saint and Greavsie* that aired on Saturday lunchtime on ITV when all matches kicked off at 3 p.m. Those were the days! Ian St John and Jimmy Greaves, legends from the Swinging Sixties, dubbed football 'a funny old game' and I fully endorse that statement. Football to me has always been about entertaining and I was privileged when football pundits likened me to Sunderland fifties' star Len Shackleton, known as the 'Clown Prince of Football'. That was good enough for little old Duncan McKenzie from Grimsby.

Okay, I was not the best of team players and failed to land the top honours but fans who saw me play, irrespective of club allegiance, still tell me today I entertained them and that will do for me. I scored my share of goals and enjoyed a terrific rapport with supporters at every club that signed me. Hearing the likes of Forest, United, Everton and Blackburn supporters chant my name was music to my ears. And three decades on from when I hung up my boots, supporters remember my football and goals so I must have done something right.

Where did it all start?

I was born in Grimsby on 10 June 1950. My parents, Francis and Elizabeth McKenzie, had a bit of a raw deal in life. Dad was one of 10 kids. He lost his mother at seven and his father at 12, so aunties and uncles brought him up. This could not have been easy and he contracted rheumatoid arthritis working at Binbrook's hanger just before the Second World War broke out. Dad went on to work for my grandfather's plumbing company as a labourer on Grimsby docks.

Mum was a Grimsby lass through and through. One of three sisters, mum was known as Betty by everyone in the neighbourhood. She was a big lady in every sense and everyone loved her fulsome approach to life. Mum worked at a butcher's shop when I was a kid and it was a struggle financially. Ironically, when I left school to join Nottingham Forest, it coincided with her being a successful businessperson, becoming regional manager for Tupperware and Board of Trade chairman for Cleethorpes.

Hard work sadly got the better of both my parents. Dad died at a young age, while mum overcame cervical cancer only to find that secondary cancer takes no prisoners, although she battled to the end. Mum and dad had a raw deal in terms of health but it never affected my childhood. Dad used to enjoy taking us for a run out in the car on a Sunday. We'd go brambling and strawberry picking. We also went to the races, which was my grandfather's favourite pastime. You name it and the McKenzie's did it.

Although money was tight for my parents, I never felt that I went without and could always rely on nan, auntie Cym and auntie Ann to spoil me rotten. I loved reading comics, especially *Dandy* and *Beano* before progressing to *The Victor*. After living without television for years we eventually got one. In 1961 we went on a first family holiday to Spain. Mum said it cost £11, which was a small fortune in those days. Mum and dad gave up a lot for me. It was wonderful, in some respects, being an only child as I got everything but it would have been nice growing up and sharing things with a brother or sister. I have fantastic childhood memories, especially of Christmas, and looking back, I pinch myself because I cannot believe how lucky I've been.

Christmas time was massive for the McKenzie clan. Everyone really looked forward to the festive period and we'd have a wonderful time. The build up was always exciting and come Christmas Day, we met up at nan's house. Auntie Cym and auntie Ann would arrive with my cousins. Sadly, the modern generation are often more mercenary and traditional family get-togethers are, in many cases, a thing of the past. It's a case of the 'me, me, me' syndrome. The wonder of Christmas has gone with the advent of global materialism, which is heartbreaking. But back in the fifties, it was a different world. All my family lived close by. In fact just a field separated our home from nan's, which seemed miles away but was actually only around 250 yards.

On Christmas Eve, I slept at nan's, who had to put up with me going through my Christmas stocking in the wee hours to see what Father Christmas had brought me. I loved getting presents and still do! For me, giving and receiving presents at a celebratory time is important. I'd get Dinky cars and the like in my formative years but in my teen years I'd get anything sports-related whether a cricket bat, football boots or a football top. At school, you had to buy a football top, so getting a new one was awesome. Sweets, something I am still partial to, especially floral gums, were a firm favourite.

When it came to Christmas lunch, forget Jamie Oliver, Gordon Ramsay and all those modern day celebrity TV chefs, nan's dinner was the dog's b******s. Everything and anything nan made was amazing—and she made all sorts—including her own bread, cakes and pickled onions. People flocked from miles around for nan's recipes. Nan would say, pointing out ingredients, 'You use a goodly amount of this, a handful of this and a smattering of this.' There was never an exact measurement in nan's recipes but it was food to die for and nan was renowned in the area for her culinary skills. People would ring my grandfather at work to order a Swiss roll cake or Bakewell tart and the orders were endless.

Nan could easily have made a cottage industry out of her talent but she came from an era when you did it as a favour and there were plenty of willing tasters. I'd often be round at nan's when she put a dough ball with a tea towel over it in front of the fire and I'd watch it rise. One day nan's terrier, Binky, stuck its nose in the dough and the next moment the dog's belly was rising along with the dough inside! Nan was not impressed with Binky but she was smiling from ear to ear.

Playing all sports was in my blood. Every day, I threw my breakfast down and could not wait to get outside and play football or cricket. Playing sport came naturally to me. I was a good cricketer, athlete and football player. And academically, I was top of the class through junior school. Life seemed easy but my junior form teacher Mr Harriman was not amused because all I ever wanted to do was play sport. My mind was not on work as my eyes were always on the sports field. And my love for sport ultimately affected me at Wintringham Grammar School. It was an excellent Grimsby school. I started in the top grade but ended up in the bottom much to the annoyance of my parents, although they didn't really give me a tough time over it.

At Wintringham, which was not a rugby school, like so many in the area, it was football all the way in wintertime. I used to go in goal for house football matches, get the ball and dribble around everyone before scoring at the other end and jog back to goal. We'd win at the last minute and I'd be the hero. I had the ability to do it but it could be difficult at times because I was not really bragging, although it may have seemed like it. At that age, it was just something I could do, just as other kids could write or do maths incredibly well. Most kids were not jealous as such because I was likeable. I still see old mates and we laugh about those carefree days.

Wintringham was an old-style academic school, teachers wore mortarboards and gowns. Famous ex-pupils include the Chancellor of the Exchequer, Norman Lamont. Academic success was paramount and the school headmaster frowned at times upon my so-called sporting prowess. But this was not going to hold me back. Grimsby was not renowned as a football hotbed like the North East or Merseyside, but Wintringham, albeit on a minor scale, produced a number of youngsters in Eric Lose, Jim and Pete McKenzie, no relation, and Keith Brown who had a shot at pro-football. None made the top flight but had talent at a young age. I was more fortunate and remain thankful for the breaks that came my way.

In the summer, action centred on the athletics track and cricket field. Dear old Ron Pickering, a great athletics coach, wanted me to take up field events but in those days, it was very much an amateur sport. There was no such thing as lottery grants for prospective stars. As a kid, I used to excel at javelin, pole vault and high jump. Pole vault only came in during my final year at school and I briefly held the county record. In the javelin, I had an incredible throwing arm for someone slightly built but failed to pressurise the top throwers, although it did lead to a party trick of chucking a cricket and golf ball long distances. Throwing is pure technique, like running reactions or striking a football. In sport, things may come naturally, but you still have to work at it even though inherently the skill is in place.

In cricket, I was one of those smart arses who could bat and bowl but I got my comeuppance on my 16th birthday when we played Nottinghamshire at schoolboy level. I opened the bowling and a young batsman put the ball straight back over my head. The ball landed in the middle of a cow field and the villain of the piece didn't even slog it. The culprit was none other than a certain Derek Randall. Of course, I've dined out many times on the back of this particular tale so I'm not complaining as 'Rags' went on to star for Notts and England at the highest level. We're still great mates, which is terrific.

I did impress enough to captain the side but there was no chance that I could develop a career twinned with football, although it was an era when you could still play both sports. A few players had successful cricket and football careers. I was not at the dual level but Chris Balderstone, another old mate, was successful in both codes, especially cricket. Chris played for

Yorkshire, Leicestershire and England while making a mark at Huddersfield Town, Carlisle United, Doncaster Rovers and Queen of the South. Signed by future Liverpool boss, legendary Bill Shankly, while he was making his name as a manager in the lower leagues, Chris had to bide his time playing first team football at Huddersfield until a certain Denis Law joined Manchester City. A left arm spin bowler and lower order batsman, Chris claimed major honours with Leicestershire and on one occasion while playing against Derbyshire at Chesterfield, at the end of play he raced to Doncaster for a football match. Chris went on to become a cricket umpire.

Ted Hemsley also enjoyed success in both sports. Best known as a first team regular at left back for Sheffield United, Ted was also a medium pace bowler for 14 seasons and part of a winning County Championship side at Worcestershire. Ted holds the unusual record of playing cricket for Worcestershire in a match against Yorkshire on his home football ground of Bramall Lane. Another star of both codes was Arnie Sidebottom who started out as a centre half of promise at Manchester United but after helping them win promotion from Division 2 in 1974–75, failed to become an established part of the Old Trafford set up. Arnie later played for Halifax Town. Cricket, though, was his forte and Arnie established himself as a regular with Yorkshire. Arnie went on to play for England and in recent years has been able to follow his son Ryan's fortunes as a top class international cricketer.

I am still fortunate that every day of my life remains sports related. Things may have been different because my apprenticeship in the game was non-existent. Dad was determined I should have an education as he worked with ex-football players who were labourers on the docks. He was being cautious but was always encouraging and as I was born south of the Humber in Lincolnshire, dad would not buy me a cricket bat. I think he had visions of me knocking centuries against his beloved Yorkshire. Football, though, would ultimately be my game and I came from good stock. Dad was a fair footballer at youth level. A skilful winger, he played at local level and was on the verge of joining Grimsby Town before rheumatoid arthritis cut his career short. Scouts watched him, but it was not to be.

Dad was a quiet man and not the type to offer praise naturally but years later, after I joined Leeds United, we chatted about his favourite players. Being a Scarborough lad, I thought he'd say legends like Len Shackleton, John Charles, Jackie Milburn or Nat Lofthouse. But Dad nominated his son, Duncan McKenzie, which stunned me somewhat. Dad was clearly proud as punch and it must have been the happiest day of his life when I signed for his favourite team.

Growing up on Weelsby Estate, Grimsby, during the early sixties meant there was a lot of freedom for a young kid. And society was a safer place. Kids in the street met up on a regular basis, as there was a magnificent playing field at the front of the estate. It was not far from the main road but there were few cars to worry about. Often at weekends, we'd play mass 40-a-side matches. All ages played. Dads joined in when they came home from work or would come out for 10 minutes during a break to have a kick around. Apart from opponents trying to hack six belles out of you at every opportunity, little girls made daisy chains on the pitch so we had to weave our way around a lot of obstacles. This probably helped me in terms of balance for mazy runs in years to come, though the likes of Chopper Harris and 'Bites Yer Legs' Hunter were not around in those days! For a football-loving kid, life was great but we had no alternatives such as Playstations, Wiis and iPods. As a teenager, the local jazz club and Rumble Band was our nightlife.

Early on in my football career, I realised talented youngsters needed handling differently. Some lads needed gentle encouragement while others needed a kick up the backside. Coaches simply yelling failed to inspire players with ability. It was insane. The fear factor would quickly set in and potential future stars were lost to the game, which was a crazy situation. Coaches were looking for resilience but not all teenagers have that at an early age. Fortunately, I had bundles of attitude and may have looked cocky but it served me well. I had an inner belief I'd make it as a professional footballer. I believed in my talent. Sergeant-major tactics, even bullying, failed to ruffle me and critics never got to me. I've always been optimistic or even rebellious when I believe I'm right. I had the arrogance of youth and brow beating never got a response from me. I believed my skills would ultimately shine through. At times, I did not endear myself to coaches but that was my personality and I'd eventually make my name.

As a mad-keen football fan, I followed the fortunes of Grimsby Town. Nicknamed the Mariners, Grimsby struggled in the main, but my memories of that era are great because it was all I knew. I was only six when Grimsby won the old Third Division North title in 1955–56 and unfortunately I don't recall anything from that season. Dad took me to watch Grimsby in the late fifties when Don Donovan, a star at Everton and the Republic of Ireland, was captain. My other Grimsby megastars were centre-forward Ron 'Chips' Rafferty who scored a stack of goals, Cliff Portwood, and outside-right Johnny Scott, who had been at the club for a number of years after he failed to break into the great Manchester United side due to the form of Busby Babe, Johnny Berry.

Grimsby suffered relegation in 1959, but three years on they gained promotion back to Division 2, which was terrific. Town came good in the second half of the campaign and a 5–3 win in the last home match against Watford, when Rafferty scored twice, sent a packed house home confident that we'd clinch the runners up spot in the final game at Brentford. Rafferty and Portwood came up trumps to end the season on a high. Rafferty knocked in 34 goals and was top scorer four out of five seasons, which was some going but his departure to Hull City was a blow and Grimsby suffered relegation again in 1964. Town were a shade unfortunate, though, as records show they went down by 0.045 of a goal.

I loved supporting Grimsby Town and still look out for their results. From the age of 10, I hitched a train ride with mates to watch away games. We'd play football in the morning and then go down to the train station. During the early sixties, we went to local games but when Grimsby enjoyed a terrific run early on in the 1965–66 season, nobody could stop us travelling to Millwall. We got a platform ticket and sneaked on the train. When the ticket inspector came along we laid flat on the luggage rack with a coat covering ourselves so as not to get caught. Eric Lose was on schoolboy forms and had a pass with no picture on. Eric went in before slipping his pass back to us through the railings. It was all innocent fun but we got it in the neck when we returned home after 10 p.m. and to make matters worse, we lost 2–1. 'What time do you call this?' mum shrieked when I finally arrived back home. She nearly killed me. But the world was a lot safer in the days when there was no segregation inside the grounds.

Like all kids, I needed heroes and Rafferty was tops with me but he could not be classed as a household name. Neither could my other Town footballing hero, Graham Taylor. Graham, who played left back, went on to manage Watford, Aston Villa and England, and now is an accomplished 5 Live summariser. Graham laughs with me every time we see each other because I was once featured in a football magazine. Under the 'favourite goal' selection, I nominated Graham with a 30-yard screamer (Grimsby Town versus Darlington, September 1967). Graham scored two goals for Town in 200 plus appearances. This was his first but he was probably trying to kick the ball out of the ground! Over the years, I took part in other such embarrassing questionnaires. I offered the following exclusives to fans in a Leeds match programme shortly after joining:

Car: Vauxhall Victor

Favourite TV Show: *Kung Fu*

Favourite Singer: Perry Como

Best Friend: My dog Sasha

Profession if not a Footballer: A deckhand on a submarine

It was all innocent fun.

Grimsby did not play glamour clubs like Manchester United and Tottenham Hotspur on a regular basis but like all football-mad kids, we pretended to be heroes of the day at the local park. We'd put our coats on the ground as posts prior to becoming Bobby Charlton, Jimmy Greaves, Derek Dougan or Denis Law. Graham Taylor had disappeared from my radar and although I admired greatly both Charlton and Greaves, being the rebellious rascal that I was, I chose not to go down the straight and narrow path because Law was making national headlines. I first saw Denis play in 1961 and his long shirtsleeves, movement and style stood out. Denis had an aura that he was better than the rest. I thought, 'Wow!'

As a kid, I'd hold my sleeves in the same way as Denis and when I scored, raise an arm up just like Denis. He was eye-catching and all these years later, is still my all-time football hero. Law and George Best made a unique trio with Bobby Charlton at Manchester United. Bobby is the most noticeable Englishman whether you look at politicians, pop stars or state figures. Bobby is lauded as a legendary player, gentleman and ambassador of the game. I never had the privilege of playing alongside either Bobby or Denis but did play alongside Bestie in a friendly. Years later, a supporter showed me the match programme and we'd both signed a picture in it. I told him it would be worth a fortune after being signed by me!

Come the 1966 World Cup, along with the whole country, I got swept up in the hysteria of the tournament as England progressed. Come the final against West Germany, I had to be at Wembley. Along with two mates, I went down to Wembley on the day, thinking we may be able to get tickets, even though we had not been to any other games. Outside the ground you could get tickets but touts wanted double the ticket price. We did not know that the stadium was not full, which is incredible when you think about it. We hung around and eventually the touts moved on none too happy. We asked a tout for tickets and he obliged. The excitement was incredible as we raced through the turnstiles and could not believe our good fortune. There was a mighty roar as we entered the stadium. At first we thought England had scored, but we were soon despondent as we were in the German end. England were a goal down and German supporters were jumping up and down. In the end, we were the ones cheering as Bobby Moore, Geoff Hurst, Bobby Charlton and the Boys of 1966 became national heroes under Alf Ramsey, as he was in those days.

Interest in the game was exploding. I remember playing in the streets and betting a mate of mine across the road that I'd be playing in the 1970 World Cup. But such dreams were a million miles away as I played for Cleethorpes Sunday pub team, Clee Rovers, against dockers and trawler men. Given half a chance, these cloggers would have kicked 10 bells out of me. Mum used to ask dad if playing at my age against these men at that level was doing me any good. Dad was not worried. He told mum not to worry, they would have to catch me first. Dad realised I had a sixth sense when it came to being tackled, even at such an early age, and I could not get enough football. I'd play Saturday morning, Saturday afternoon, Sunday morning, Sunday afternoon and midweek but that was normal for kids of my age. I had to be swift on my feet and further developed my dribbling skills.

I was nifty on my feet, despite having proper football boots, though comfort was far from important in the design. I was proud of my first pair of football boots because Stanley Matthews of Blackpool and England fame endorsed them. The studs, like today, came separately but you had to nail them in. Afterwards you sat in the bath because they crippled you and blood would stream from your feet. Mum would say, 'Are they all right?'

Through gritted teeth I'd say, 'Yeh great', because I was frightened that if I complained that would be it. My boots were a very special present. Dad came home with them one day. His weekly wage packet was only something like 15 shillings and I thought, 'God almighty this is amazing'.

Father Canning, who coached Notre Dame, loved football and ran Under-9 to Under-16 teams. He spotted me playing for Old Clee and I was soon making my name for his Notre Dame side. We went all over the UK to play games and I recall playing in matches against sides from Dublin, Scotland and Jersey. We also faced Tottenham Hotspur Boys. Spurs boss Bill Nicholson signed up one of our players, Neil Johnson, who went on to play in a famous game when Tottenham defeated Manchester United 5–1 as the match was televised on BBC's *Match of the Day* (then in its infancy as a programme). Jimmy Greaves dribbled around the entire team before scoring one of a hat-trick of goals. That day Neil played right wing and scored. Tottenham lost the reverse fixture 5–1.

Father Canning had an eye for spotting talented young footballers and his Notre Dame Sunday League teams had plenty of skills. I played in the morning for Old Clee and for Notre Dame in the afternoon. Going through the ranks, I played for my school and local clubs but no representative honours came my way before joining Nottingham Forest. The football network in those days seemed to cover major clubs but not unfashionable Grimsby Town. Tottenham and Arsenal showed interest but nothing materialised. Sadly, although many teams have academies, nothing has really altered my perception that talent is missed because of poor scouting networks around the country. Often, big boys of the English game miss kids impressing at small-town clubs. A number of comics on the after-dinner circuit quip that Grimsby is twinned with Grimsby when it comes to kids breaking through. I know it's tongue in cheek because Grimsby is a terrific town based in one of the prettiest counties but it's not really the place to be for getting spotted. I had trials at Grimsby but wasn't eight foot tall! The Grimsby Boys team was huge. Joking apart, Grimsby decided not to come in for me so my progress was slow, but I could not help that situation, it's just the way it worked out.

I was still at school when my break came. Notre Dame faced a Nottingham Forest junior XI. Roly Abrams was a part-time scout for Forest and was impressed enough to ask me to attend a trial match. I was still shocked when an invite arrived through the post. It was a massive thing for a kid. Unfortunately I twisted an ankle so was out for six weeks but, despite the disappointment, Forest asked me to attend training on a Thursday for a month. I got fit and dad drove me to Forest 'A' team games and then took me back home afterwards.

With Christmas approaching, no offer was forthcoming and

it was a frustrating time. It got to a point where I thought that Forest would continue playing me as an amateur if I let them. I decided to confront club officials. Bracing myself, I picked my moment and put forward my case to Bill Anderson, Johnny Carey's right-hand man. It was a risky strategy but it paid off. I had no idea if it was my football ability or direct attitude that impressed Bill, but Forest signed me on as a ground staff boy.

I was delighted that I'd been headstrong, but I had an ally in Wintringham headmaster Norman Havard, who told me to have a go and that if I didn't, the chance may disappear. He knew my dad wanted me to get a sensible trade but said, 'Leave your dad to me.' Norman pointed out if it did not work at least I'd tried, but he was confident I'd be more than good enough. He just had this feeling and I had a lot to thank him for when I joined Forest. I was a late developer in terms of getting into football so knew it was not going to be easy initially, but I often look back because it was a defining period in my football career. It could have gone one way or another. I decided to avoid work and give football a go.

I left school at Christmas with 10 'O' levels in terms of qualifications. There was also the possibility of returning to school to further my education and take up a respectable career path if it did not work out at Forest. Mum bought me a Morris Minor for £50, which was a small fortune. Everything about the car was dicky. Mum also got me a second hand suit from one of her bosses at Tupperware. Mum knew I needed a suit and it was a big outlay for her on both counts. I thought to myself, Nottingham Forest here I come. Forest gave me a chance and I will always be grateful for that opportunity. Before Forest, I'd only played local football. Irony of ironies, the day after I put pen to paper, Lincolnshire County selected me. More importantly, I knew that it was down to me to make the most of my opportunity at Forest. This was my chance and I was determined to make it.

2

TRACTOR BOY, FOREST FIRE AND ROKER ROAR

Nottingham Forest were a club on a high when I began my career at the City Ground, Christmas 1967. Forest were challenging for the Division 1 title and ultimately finished runners-up to Manchester United who had Bobby Charlton, Denis Law and George Best starring for them. United also had the likes of Bill Foulkes and Nobby Stiles. Tottenham Hotspur finished third on goal average. In the FA Cup, Forest fell at the semi-final stage to Tottenham at Hillsborough when Jimmy Greaves knocked in two goals. Bill Nicholson's team defeated Chelsea 2–1 in the final and Forest felt it was a case of what might have been, especially as they enjoyed their best season before the Cloughie era began.

Johnny Carey was Forest boss. You would never see Johnny in a tracksuit and his style was always courteous. Johnny dressed in a suit all year round, adding a coat to his attire in the winter. He was very much from the old school when it came to management. His assistant, Bill Anderson, and trainer, Tommy Cavanagh, did all the barking and screaming, while Johnny walked to training a couple of times a week, watched studiously and then advised the lads to fizz the ball about whenever possible. Even before a game Johnny was his gentle self. Of course, there were instructions on who to mark and so on, but for Johnny it was a case of putting an arm around a player for encouragement rather than screaming. His management style proved to be successful.

Scottish international Jim Baxter starred at Rangers before joining Forest from Sunderland in a £100,000 deal which, in the late sixties, was seen as a small fortune. To the media boys, Slim Jim was the main man but in reality he was past his best at the top level. Joe Baker was another past star at the end of an illustrious career but on the park was a shadow of himself in his pomp. Both transfers generated plenty of headlines and they were popular with fans at the Trent End. Joe was 'The King' while Jim was known as the 'Mighty Jim' from the classic 'Mighty Quin' song.

More influential players included Ian Storey-Moore, Frank Wignall, Henry Newton, Terry Hennessey and Peter Cormack, who later thrilled Liverpool fans. Forest had a strong squad because they also had Peter Grummitt, John Winfield and Bob McKinlay available. The main striker was Storey-Moore. A terrific player, Ian was undoubtedly one of the first team stars, but suffered in the popular press because he did not play for a city slicker club. As a winger, Ian scored for fun but only picked up a handful of England caps, which was ludicrous. Cloughie tried to take him to Derby County when he was manager but Forest weren't going to do business, especially when he attempted to parade him through the press as a nailed on deal. Eventually Ian joined Manchester United where an ankle injury curtailed his career.

In the dressing room, Sammy Chapman and John 'Bill' Brindley were forever pulling stunts. Sammy started off as a schoolboy inside forward but was moved into defence and found his niche as an uncompromising centre half. Bill played right full back and moved across the water to join neighbours Notts County. At the time it was seen as a bit of a move down but he was great to have around. A typical barrow boy character, Bill was chirpy and always had something to say.

Playing for the first XI was not on my radar as I settled down to life as a member of the ground staff. There was a feel-good factor at training when the club was going well and I trained with the first team squad. Away from the City Ground, I lived in digs locally with Billy Styles, Alan Buckley, Graham Collier, Dave Serella, John Robertson, Jimmy McCaffrey and Maitland Pollock. We were all just kids growing up and got up to plenty of pranks. When players first joined Forest, there was an initiation ceremony of getting dunked in a cold bath. It was all harmless fun.

As ground staff players we all had various jobs to do before and after training. These jobs aimed to build character prior to possibly becoming a part of the glitzy world of first team football. We came in before professional players in the first team squad to prepare boots and training gear before joining the senior lads for training. We also helped weed the pitch for the groundsman and swept the terraces (this latter chore offered us a bonus of making a small fortune as we found as much money on the terraces as we received in our wages). Whatever we found, we shared, but Health and Safety officials would shudder. We put all the garbage in big containers at the back of the ground behind the East Stand and burnt the waste as we choked at times on the fumes. I quickly became an environmental expert!

Although I was willing, some of the other lads were far more conscientious when it came to mucking in with the tasks. One day, Tommy was not happy with my attitude and let me know in no uncertain manner during training. 'Aye aye Sonny Jim with your fancy tricks, dancing feet and dribbling skills around people before scoring goals!' he yelled. 'You may be doing it in the third team lad, but you won't do it in the reserves.' When I did, Tommy pushed me more. 'Aye aye Sonny Jim, you may be doing it in the reserves but you won't be doing it in the first team.' I was not sure what to think. Was Tommy being serious or just pushing me?

One task I did enjoy was driving the playing field tractor. This did not impress Tommy as it was deemed to be a cushy number. More to the point, Tommy was not enamoured with my efforts cleaning first team boots either. Not for the first time, I was hauled up in front of the boss who put me in my place. I took it on the chin but found other spats simply petty. One such occasion was when I got rollicked for walking across Trent Bridge cricket ground at midnight eating a packet of salt and vinegar crisps. Bill Anderson was livid and made it abundantly clear that my conduct was not conducive to making it as a professional footballer. I felt miffed by the incident, but in hindsight Bill was trying to steer me on the right path.

Tommy and I clashed on numerous occasions. He was a real taskmaster, and his training style did not suit me. Don't get me wrong, I trained hard but Tommy continually appeared unhappy with what he dubbed my 'laid-back attitude'. I liked a joke and enjoyed a crack with the lads, but at times Tommy was not impressed with my approach. To me it was just banter but Tommy made it clear that I was trouble and would be on my way out of Forest permanently or put on loan unless I bucked up my ideas. I was still only a kid but he wanted me to toe the club line.

A disciplinarian and rollicking machine, Tommy was from the old school and wanted footballers to be 100 percent committed. To Tommy, image was an essential part of being a professional footballer. He wanted us dressed smartly, clean-shaven with short hair. Ground staff lads needed discipline and I was no exception. A number of lads failed to adapt and moved on. Even though we clashed, I stayed on at Forest. We did get on in the end, although Tommy had little choice as I married his goddaughter! I was in the reserves when I first met Dot, who came to visit her brother, fellow ground staff lad Billy Styles. Dot and I got married at St George's Church in Liverpool. The vicar was a massive Red so there was plenty of banter at the ceremony as I was marrying into an Evertonian family. Being married to Dot, though, brought no favours from Tommy, who was still hard to please in training, but at least he was a tad more complimentary away from the City Ground.

All the lads had different personalities and let off steam in different ways. Getting into scrapes was all part of growing up. Generally we could not get up to many pranks with first team players. On the whole we did as we were told and gaffs were at our peril. I was quick to learn.

During a five-a-side game in training, I could not stop myself nut-megging Sammy Chapman when the opportunity arose. I knew instantly that it was a big mistake as Sammy squared up to the new upstart on the block. Sammy was on a short fuse at the best of times and was not going to be usurped by me making him the butt of a joke. I thought to myself, 'McKenzie you've bitten off more than you can chew', but I was determined to go down fighting. I hit Sammy with my best shot before being carted off from one blow. I ended up in the physio's room. The doc just shrugged his shoulders, 'Daft fool McKenzie, when are you going to learn?'

Around this period, I gained a reputation for picking up a few bob on the side courtesy of being able to hurdle over a five-foot bar gate with a bit of barbed wire on top. We trained around the back of the Boots training ground. There was a little turnstile by the side of the gate and after training the lads would queue up to go through. To save time, I'd jump over the obstacle. I didn't put my hand on to vault, I just hurdled the gate cleanly. The lads looked at me aghast but to me it was nothing because I knew that I could do it. I'd cleared this sort of height easily during my school high jump days.

One day after training, Forest reserve keeper Brian Williamson said that Tommy Cavanaugh's car was lower than the bar gate and dared me to jump it for a fiver. Not earning a fortune and knowing that I could not lose. I accepted the challenge and, to his astonished looks, I wheeled around before jumping clean over the car. Of course, footballers being footballers, I didn't get the fiver but my fellow apprentices clicked and relieved many an unsuspecting punter of a few quid. Alan Buckley always felt the most amazing sight was when I cleared the top of Joe Baker's Jag.

When learning the game, we found time to get up to plenty of mischief as a group. When Forest travelled to Old Trafford for a game against Manchester United, nobody knew the apprentices, not even our own coach driver. We went to the team bus and started chatting to him. While the driver was sidetracked, a number of the apprentices nicked the basket containing the first team's strip and we were soon carrying it to the dressing room before running down the tunnel and over the wall to watch the game. You would not get away with that now.

Of all the lads, Dave Serella was an absolute scream, but at times a bit of a nutcase. Dave could be outrageous. Nothing fazed him. He was fearless and a real personality in the dressing room. Dave would think nothing of climbing up a floodlight pylon before hanging on it and swinging with one arm. He repeated the mind-boggling act by swinging off the Trent Bridge. One slip and he could have been a goner in the River Trent, but that was Dave and his antics kept us amused. I was also thick as thieves with Dermot O'Shea, who had joined from Manchester United. Dermot lived near Dublin and, during a weekend break to his hometown, with us not having vast finances available, walked 14 miles to Bray to see the Dixie Showband before walking 14 miles back home. They were mad days but thoroughly enjoyable.

Not everyone made it in the professional game among the apprentices. We all knew that the majority of us would not make the grade. As at all other clubs, most would fall by the wayside. I hoped I would be one of the lucky ones. Despite inherent pressure, the atmosphere was terrific. As the oldest among the rookies, I tried to negotiate a day off for the lads with the boss. Forest boss Johnny Carey listened to my point of view and then in his beautiful Irish lilt explained his reasoning as to why we did not get our wish. Johnny asked me what we did on a Monday to Friday. I said, 'Play football.' Johnny then asked what we did on a Saturday. I said, 'Play football.' Johnny finally asked what I wanted to do most in the world. Naturally, I said, 'Play football.' I fell right into the trap. Johnny said that if he gave us time off we would not be able to play football on those days. I left his office snookered with nothing but a smile on my face. Johnny had bamboozled me with his silver Irish tongue.

The ground staff lads experienced varying football careers. Martin O'Neill and John Robertson played international football for Northern Ireland and Scotland, respectively. They also enjoyed huge success at Forest, winning the European Cup among numerous honours. Martin and John have since teamed up at Aston Villa. Liam O'Kane also gained international honours then became a physio. Alan Buckley went into management, John Cottam joined the Metropolitan Police while Jim McCaffrey, my best mate and best man when I married Dot, played for Mansfield Town. Graham Collier went on to play for

Leicester City.

It was obvious, even in those distant days, that Martin O'Neill had clear beliefs about his playing ability and thoughts on the game that would develop into his management style. For some reason, Martin was not a confident footballer but you could see he had true talent and Cloughie would bring that to the fore. As a manager, Martin is among the best in the country. His man-management skills shine through. Martin brought massive success to Leicester City and Celtic and now has stamped his mark at Villa.

Results dipped after a fine start by the first team in 1967–68 before Forest finished the campaign in 11th place. Injuries to Storey-Moore and Barnwell demonstrated the club's lack of squad strength, which was why the club needed a successful youth policy. My attitude in the formative months did not go down particularly well overall with the managerial hierarchy but my demeanour at times was down to sheer frustration as there seemed no sniff of first team action. Also I felt annoyed about my wages. Unlike other ground staff lads, I'd signed a non-playing contract, as I was a few months off my 18th birthday. When I turned professional in July 1968, I received a £250 signing on fee while my basic weekly wage rose from £7 to £12. It was pitiful in my view. I knew I'd have to prove myself before I received a bigger pay rise.

While the first team players departed for a summer break, as a young professional, I helped the groundsman weed and touch up the terraces around the ground. I also had my cushy number on the tractor, which whiled away the time. We only had a fortnight off, whereas senior pros were off for the distance. It was far from a glamorous lifestyle but I was not complaining. Being at the ground during the close season did have its compensations because legendary West Indies cricketer Garfield

Sobers was in his pomp at Trent Bridge. At the time 'Rags' Randall was at Nottinghamshire making his way in the game and it was not long before I became the bookies' runner. Known as something of a speed merchant, I'd be despatched to find out when Gary Sobers was in. We'd quickly curtail training to see the great man at the crease.

Come the 1968–69 season, just one win before December resulted in Johnny Carey paying the price with his job. Panic had set in amongst the directors. Some things have not changed in football! Bill Anderson became caretaker manager before Matt Gillies took the helm within a few weeks. Matt had led Leicester City to two FA Cup finals and a League Cup triumph so had standing in the game. It quickly became clear that players needed to be approaching 30 or beyond to have a chance of getting into his first XI on a regular basis.

My lack of first team football opportunities was getting me down but I was making an impression with some of the senior lads. Ronnie Rees, who joined from Coventry City and played for Wales, went to see Matt. With Forest struggling for form and deep in a relegation battle, Ronnie asked Matt to throw me into the first team. He believed that I'd offer something different to the side. Ronnie described me as a physical freak as I could jump over cars, throw a ball long distances and run all day. Also he was impressed that whenever defenders hoofed the old heavy football high into the sky and it came down with snow on, I'd instantly trap it. The ball never hit the deck. Ronnie told Matt that while I was full of tricks, I had more to my game. In practice games, when on song, none of the lads could get near me and they struggled to get the ball from me when I was in possession. Ronnie likened me to a grasshopper as I was constantly on the move, but it was to no avail. I'd have to bide my time. Forest avoided relegation in 1968–69 thanks to a string of wins through the crucial Easter fixtures but it had been a narrow escape.

Although out of the frame for first team football, I did enjoy the atmosphere of a big game at the City Ground. There was a hairy moment early on in the season (24 August 1968) when Alan Buckley and I almost got trapped in the infamous Forest fire during a clash against Leeds United. The match was abandoned at half time and luckily there were no fatalities.

Bucks and I were young professionals watching the game from our usual vantage point in the players' pen by the side of the tunnel where the teams ran out. Our duties as part of the backroom team were to be available should players need drinks, to put new studs in boots and so on. A few minutes before half time, we went to the home dressing room to make sure everything was set out in terms of cups of tea, water and the like. As we made our way to the boot room, suddenly the pair of us were in the midst of smoke. It was obvious there was something amiss. Unbeknown to us a fire had started upstairs and smoke engulfed the corridors of the building. I put my white synthetic training coat over my head, Bucks grabbed the back of my coat and followed me along the wall towards the fire door that opened out on to the car park. Above us, the corrugated roof at the back of the stand was ablaze. Flames were everywhere and sparks were flying down. A copper yelled for us to get back inside but we shouted back, 'No way!' He had no idea what was behind the door as we put our coats over our heads and legged it away from the ground. Neither of us has ever run so fast in our lives.

The alarm was raised and club officials, together with police, evacuated supporters in the stands on to the pitch. The stand was gutted and out of action for some time. Players used the Trent Bridge cricket ground to get changed before making their way to the pitch. Eventually, a new stand was erected. Looking back at an old newspaper report at the time in the pre-match build up, the headline unwittingly predicted the outcome. 'Leeds to set Forest Ablaze!'

During this period, nothing seemed to be going my way. Then I began to discover that Tommy Cavanagh, in an indirect way, through his constant pushing thought I could make the grade as a professional footballer. One day during training, a trainee hoping for an opportunity was having a nightmare on the park. I expected Tommy to rollick him but Tommy put his arm around him and offered words of encouragement. Tommy let the trainee get changed and told me shortly afterwards that Forest were letting him go. There was no point having him at Forest for a year and making his life a misery. I realised Tommy was saying, in effect, 'McKenzie, you can play son.'

Tommy was looking for mental strength. I could not fault him for that, but when it came to training techniques, Tommy was no coaching guru. Matt brought in former Charlton Athletic defender Bert Johnson, a wily old character with wonderful ways. Bert quickly rejuvenated training. Whereas Tommy would have 40 players lined up on the halfway line before running around the pitch against the clock at 10-second intervals, Bert had us doing laps two seconds apart. With his psychological outlook, Bert realised a player at the front did not want to be caught by a player behind, and the player behind did not want to get caught by the next player, and so on. Players were pushing themselves to the limit. Bert quickly found the fastest and slowest runners. He changed the order to suit the sprinting ability of all the lads. Tommy was impressed, but not best pleased, as he could not rollick anyone on a regular basis.

Training was basic for footballers in the fifties and sixties but there were exceptions. Before my era, Stanley Matthews of Blackpool and England fame, preferred not to train with his colleagues. Stan trained by himself on Blackpool beach, running through sand dunes and the sea because he felt it strengthened his calf muscles and gave him more stamina. Stan was probably right. For me training and coaching methods were mainly hit or miss. Training was great if you were part of a winning football team, but in my era it was mainly endurance work. Endurance training made sense because players had to be fit due to the pitches we played on, especially compared to today's surfaces, which often resemble a snooker table. I'd love to see Ronaldo, Robinho or Rooney ply their silky skills at the Baseball Ground.

We played practice matches which generally saw the first team outwit the reserves, but these matches gave the reserves a chance to shine. Most clubs had a similar set up but training techniques were different. At Mansfield, Jock Basford, who had his hair parted down the middle and brylcreemed to death, would waddle into the middle of the dressing room. Looking at us with menace, Jock would shout out, 'Lads give me eight, six, four, two, one!' Off we'd go and he'd disappear for a cup of tea. The first time I heard this, I looked over to Johnny Quigley as we ran out on to the pitch, and asked what he meant. Johnny was the old man on the block. An experienced player, Johnny had played in Forest's FA Cup winning team in 1959. He explained that Jock meant eight sprints, four sprints halfway round the ground, two laps and a double lap. Johnny whispered for me not to run too bloody quickly. We'd finish the exercise and kick a football against the wall round the back of the main stand. Johnny was a real character and had some great tales. One anecdote I still re-tell on the after-dinner circuit in the Nottingham area was when Forest won the Cup. After initial celebrations at the final whistle, the lads made their way over to the Royal Box for the trophy presentation. The club trainer was waiting at the bottom of the steps with a tea towel containing the players' false teeth. The lads put their teeth back in quick-sharp before walking up to receive their medals.

But thoughts of winner's medals were just pipe dreams as I tried to make my way in the game. My concerns centred on more mundane matters such as making sure my kit was up to date. Salaries did not stretch far and we had to pay the balance for any kit costing over £10. It was mind-blowing when I think back. When new-style boots came out at £14, I had to find £4. This was a lot when I only earned £12 a week. Fortunately, we have progressed since those distant days.

I was pleased with my progress but desperate for a first team break as the 1969–70 campaign approached. I impressed in both the third team and reserves so hoped for an opportunity. My chance to shine came out of the blue as Forest prepared for a clash at Sunderland in September 1969. But the manner of my call up was bizarre. On the morning of the match, Barry Lyons fell ill. I'd arrived at the ground to check the boots for the first team lads when suddenly, reserve team trainer Frank Knight said, 'All the best today young feller.'

I said, 'Thanks, but why?' Before Frank could answer, someone else wished me well. I had no idea what was happening until I was handed a suit for the trip to Sunderland. Stunned, I rushed home to change and ran back to the City Ground.

I'd wished for, and dreamed about, this moment since signing for the club but now it was here, I had no time to prepare myself. Fortuitously, I had no time to get nervous and travelled down with the first team for my professional debut. The lads gave me plenty of encouragement, telling me to go out, get an early touch and enjoy the experience. Lining up, Ian Storey-Moore moved to right wing, meaning that I'd face Cecil Irwin. Among the opposition were also Jim Montgomery, Charlie Hurley, Len Ashurst, John O'Hare and Bobby Kerr. Changing for the game, I was anxious but one thing I did not have to worry about was the

Roker Roar, as the crowd was nowhere near a sell out. Despite this, 16,000 plus supporters was the largest attendance I'd performed in front of in my life.

After getting a first touch, I just concentrated on my game. I had a few neat touches and tried to do the simple things but I got Henry Newton carried off after playing a hospital ball, which did not go down too well with the Forest lads. Henry, especially, was not pleased. For me, though, it was a memorable occasion even though we lost 2–1. Back in the dressing room there was a fiver in my boot. I asked the lads to whom it belonged and they all laughed. I quickly caught on as it was for me. I was green as grass but Happy as Larry.

I didn't get another opportunity to play for the first team during the season but, having had a taste of first team action, I knew that playing the game professionally was what I wanted more than anything else. Facing Sunderland had whetted my appetite for more. I was more determined than ever to play against the likes of Charlton, Moore, Greaves, Bremner, Best and Law, but before then I'd have to make my mark in the Central League where crowds were sparse. Despite the lack of atmosphere we did come up against international stars on occasion. I was certainly up for a home clash against a Manchester United side that included European Cup winners Foulkes, Stiles and Aston in the line-up. For me this was a step up in class and I raised my game. We drew 1–1 and I scored Forest's goal so was pleased with my efforts.

Even in my formative years as a player, I was seen as something of a Fancy Dan. The flicks and tricks came naturally and I loved entertaining supporters. Ball skills were a part of my game, whether balancing a ball on my head, catching it on my instep or juggling it with both feet. It was second nature but such skills did not really impress the Forest hierarchy. It was frustrating because I knew that I was capable of scoring on a regular basis given the opportunity. I needed a run in the first team but at the time could only dream of being part of three £200,000 transfer deals and playing at great stadia against household names.

3

EASTER THRILLS, STAGS STRIKES AND SUPERMAC

Towards the end of the 1969–70 season rumours started in the local press that I was to be given a free transfer. Interested clubs included Cambridge United, who appeared willing to part with £15,000 for my services. Leicester City were also keen, but no offer was forthcoming. A number of the older pros at Forest advised me not to be too hasty. The overall viewpoint was that I should not jump into a permanent move to a lower league club, however much I wanted to get away for regular first team action. I knew the lads made sense. A loan move would be better. I'd get first team football and have a chance to build my confidence.

An opportunity suddenly arrived when Forest needed a goalkeeper on loan after Alan Hill broke an elbow. Dave Hollins joined from Division 3 outfit Mansfield Town while I went in the opposite direction. I was delighted to get away. Still only 19, I needed a break and was determined to impress Stags manager Tom Eggleston. The loan spell was just the tonic I needed but I had to wait my turn as Mansfield were on an unbeaten run after being knocked out of the FA Cup by Leeds United. I eventually made my Mansfield debut as a substitute in a 2–0 win at home to Barnsley. Following another couple of substitute appearances,

Tom told me I'd be playing in a clash against Southport at Field Mill. It was headline news in local papers. I scored twice in a 5–0 win. The opposition was not Manchester United, Liverpool or Leeds United but I was playing first team football, scoring goals and it felt terrific.

Rotherham United led the table when we faced them in the next match. I notched another goal. My confidence was sky high. The loan spell was until the end of the season and I was earning more at Mansfield with bonuses than I had been at Forest. I didn't manage another goal but I'd struck three times in 10 appearances and by the end of my spell, Tom wanted to sign me full time, but I recalled my conversation with the lads and knew I could play at a higher level. In any case, Forest didn't want to release me so it was time to return.

Back at Forest for the start of our 1970–71 campaign, I thought I'd get a first team chance, but was wide of the mark as Matt Gillies put me in the A team. I was not even in the reserves. I felt let down by Matt. I was earning less than at Mansfield, but decided to battle away. If a reaction in training was what Matt wanted then I'd provide it. Before long I was in the reserve side and soon made the first team substitute bench. I enjoyed a few run outs but my career seemed to be stop-start. Come Easter, however, another break arrived with the team struggling and desperate for points. We had crunch games over Easter in a five-day period coming up against Manchester City, West Ham and Arsenal. It was an exciting prospect as I'd be able to pit my wits against top defenders.

On Good Friday, Matt made his changes for the side to face Manchester City at Maine Road. As Matt was resting Peter Cormack and Barry Lyons, I came in for Cormack, and Tommy Jackson replaced Lyons. We went into the clash as underdogs but, on a day to remember, I scored twice in a 3–1 win. Tommy scored our other goal. My first goal came from a right wing cross. Neil Martin went up with Tommy Booth shoulder to shoulder and the ball went between them towards me. I headed goalwards. City skipper Tony Book, who always stood on the line, volleyed the ball straight into my face and the rebound went into the back of the net. A goal to the good, the game turned even more in our favour when City keeper Ron Healey was carried off with an injury and Francis Lee went in goal. Reserve keepers on the bench were years away. From a left wing corner, I took City by surprise by leaping for the ball. City players had not heard of me so never dreamt I was spring-heeled. I got above everybody and headed home. Just as I headed the ball, Lee caught me, but could not prevent the goal. I was delighted and ran off to celebrate.

There was no way I could forget my first league goals for Nottingham Forest but my joy was immediately dashed as Tommy Jackson kept his place while the boss dropped me for our West Ham clash, stating I was tired. I was stunned by Matt's decision and not just because I could not face England skipper Bobby Moore. Some of the lads asked Matt to make me substitute, at least they had faith, but he refused to bend. I was disconsolate and wondered what I had to do for a fair opportunity.

Players moan nowadays about playing too many games, something I have no sympathy for at all. Over an Easter weekend we played Friday, Saturday and Monday. Crowds were bumper and it was a terrific atmosphere. We went on to defeat West Ham 1–0 with Storey-Moore scoring the winner. Tommy Jackson and I both missed a 3–0 home defeat to Arsenal but played the final four games of the season, which included a 3–2 win at Blackpool and close defeats against Liverpool, Stoke City and Leeds United. The Blackpool win eased any danger of relegation as

Forest ended the season in 16th spot.

I'd played nine games, five coming in the final weeks of the season. Although I'd made just a few appearances, I'd faced the likes of Liverpool hard man Tommy Smith and Leeds stopper Norman Hunter, who also had a fierce reputation, for the first time. Both were noted for being among the hardest players around in the game but I was more taken aback by 'Big' Jack Charlton. What a moaner. Whilst Norman said very little, Jack did not stop moaning throughout the game. On the day, we got battered.

I had broken into the Forest team for the first time with a run of games, but throughout the close season, wondered whether this was my break. I felt regular first team football was truly around the corner and quickly got my answer as I started the following season in the first team. Finally, I seemed to be getting somewhere. Breaking into the side, I was a bit overawed but settled down after grabbing my opening goal of the campaign against Crystal Palace in a 1–1 draw. Facing star names was something to contend with and they did not come much bigger in terms of keepers than Gordon Banks of Stoke City, who in the next match pulled off a great fingertip save from a bullet header to deprive me of a goal. I soon got over the fact I was playing against world stars and began to make a mark. A brace helped see off Aldershot in the League Cup while another strike earned a draw with Chelsea before we bowed out in the replay at Stamford Bridge.

I notched another equaliser, this time at home to pace-setters Manchester City in a 2–2 draw, but our form was poor, and indeed only one victory came our way in the opening third of the season when a Storey-Moore penalty accounted for West Ham. Struggling in the relegation zone, I was delighted to knock in our third goal during a 4–1 defeat of West Brom who had a useful side. Unfortunately, I picked up an injury in the next fixture, a 2–1 defeat at Newcastle United that would keep me sidelined, bar one brief appearance, for three months. I could not believe my misfortune.

Being injured is always frustrating and even more so when your side is struggling to find form in the bottom two. With interest in the FA Cup gone at the third round stage, following a shock exit to Millwall, a match I missed, all attention was on survival. My return to the fray against West Brom came during a wretched run of seven consecutive defeats. Our situation appeared hopeless with Forest seven points adrift from safety. These were the days when you got two points for a win so we had to pull four games back against our rivals for the drop that included Huddersfield Town, Crystal Palace and Southampton. The manager tried to boost confidence but it was a tough task. Forest battled at the Hawthorns but we went down to a solitary goal.

With Easter fixtures coming up, at last we scraped a 2–1 win at Chelsea courtesy of two goals by new signing Tommy Gemmell. I found the target in a 4–2 defeat at West Ham before notching our final goal in a 4–0 home victory over Coventry City. Tommy had seen and done it all at Celtic and Matt hoped he could add a touch of experience, but it was a tough ask. Seven games remained and although we had reduced the deficit to four points, all our rivals had games in hand. A 6–1 thumping at Leeds United, a result matched by Tottenham earlier in the season, completed a miserable Easter and demonstrated we were facing an ever-more daunting task. Leeds boss Don Revie came into our dressing room to shake our hands and wish us well. Don singled out our younger players in and around the first team such as Martin O'Neill and felt that Forest were on the right track. The sentiment was appreciated but not quite what we wanted to hear.

The final games brought victories over Newcastle United and Stoke City but it was to no avail. Two draws in our final three games confirmed relegation. Finishing second bottom, the lads were bitterly disappointed and relegation meant change at the club, but I was not fazed. Despite going down, I'd proved I could mix it with the top sides and enjoyed the pressure of top-flight football. I'd played 36 league and cup matches and scored 10 goals to finish behind Ian Storey-Moore (14 goals) in the scoring stakes. It was not the number I'd have liked, but rather the fact that I was in the scoring charts for the first time in what had been a tough season for the club.

Although I had only just made the leap into first team football on a regular basis, I'd discovered that there was something special about playing big Northern clubs away from home. The atmosphere at St James Park, Goodison Park, Maine Road and Elland Road was for real, and I knew that when I eventually ran out at Old Trafford and Anfield, I'd not be disappointed. Generally there was not the same fervency from home support in London but after playing in a huge clash, whether home or away, against clubs like Manchester United, Arsenal, Liverpool, Chelsea, Tottenham, Leeds, Everton or Manchester City, if say Coventry, Stoke or Southampton were next, the sense of expectancy was not on the same scale for either players or supporters. Big gates generate big atmospheres and big attendances. As a footballer it's human nature to have a desire to play the big boys and nothing has changed in the modern game. In the Premiership and Champions League, fixtures have a pecking order. For Ronaldo, Rooney, Fabregas, Gerrard, Torres, Lampard and Terry, facing each other domestically is greater. When playing in Europe, taking on Real Madrid, Inter Milan and Barcelona is more appealing than playing Besiktas, Werder

Bremen or Slavia Prague.

During pre-season, the general feeling in the camp was that we'd make a good start come the 1972–73 campaign and be in contention for promotion from the off. And after a couple of draws, consecutive wins over Oxford United, Brighton and Carlisle United buoyed up the lads. I notched a double to account for Carlisle United while Martin O'Neill was on target when we defeated Cardiff City, but the victory was the sole triumph in a nine-match spell. With pressure mounting, it was no shock when Matt Gillies resigned.

While the board pondered our next manager, Bill Anderson took over as caretaker-boss once again. News that Dave Mackay was to become manager went down well among the lads because here was an individual who gained instant respect even though he was starting out in management. Dave had a fantastic reputation as a player, earning honours galore at Hearts and Tottenham before ending his career by helping Derby County win the Division 2 title prior to taking on the role of player-manager at Swindon Town.

When the Forest opportunity came along Dave jumped at it, but our form continued to dip. Dave had nothing against me, far from it, but he bought John Galley from Bristol City to play alongside Neil Martin up front. We now had two giants in attack. Dave wanted Martin and me to play on the flanks but we weren't out and out wingers, which is what he had in his mind. I hit the target in a 4–0 win over Coventry City just before Christmas but struggled to make an impact on the left. By February, I was on my way to Mansfield Town for a second spell on loan. I was not happy at the thought of playing football in Division 4, but at the time there was no alternative.

Danny Williams had succeeded Tom Eggleston as Stags manager when my old mate Jim McCaffrey told Danny to come in for me. Danny brought me in to get goals and help Mansfield push for promotion. It was a long way from Anfield, Highbury and Old Trafford, but I knuckled down in the first training session and Danny gave an immediate boost in backing my talent. It took a couple of games to get used to my new teammates but a striker thrives on chances and they came my way aplenty. Following a strike in a 5–1 win over Crewe Alexandra, I was on target in a defeat at Southport, before a brace helped overcome Workington and a hat-trick versus Bradford City, the first of my professional career, claimed the spoils. My strikes pushed Mansfield into promotion contention. Dave Mackay saw me banging in the goals, seven in six games, and soon had me back on the short journey to Nottingham. The move would prove to be just the confidence booster I needed.

Dave was delighted because I'd looked out of sorts at Forest, but it did not surprise me because I was playing in my natural striking position at Mansfield. I felt comfortable. Danny Williams was a real down-to-earth character and knew the score. He was pleased to see me do well and realised that my form would mean a return to Forest sooner rather than later. My absence would probably hinder his own team's chances of promotion and his worst fears eventually transpired as Mansfield endured a poor run and slipped out of contention for promotion. At the time, Danny was not happy but wished me well as I returned to Forest.

At last, I really felt wanted at Nottingham Forest. Dave said, 'Duncan get out there and do for me what you did at Mansfield and I'll give you the chance to play.' All I wanted was to be the floating player and do my own thing. Dave put me straight back in the first team and I scored three goals in the remaining games. Forest ended the campaign in 14th place, which was not noteworthy in terms of success, but for me it was a breakthrough season.

Come the 1973–74 campaign, our squad had a mix of solid professionals and young lads making their way in the game. Jim Barron was in goal. In the dressing room, not only would Jim always be mentally prepared for a match, but also made sure he looked the part. The lads used to rib him rotten that he spent most of his time in front of the mirror. After a match or training session, Jim was last out of the dressing room, and departing for a game, was last on the coach, but we knew he was coming because we could smell his after-shave. On the field, though, is where it mattered and Jim was a great shot stopper, commanding his penalty area brilliantly.

Peter Hindley was from the old school of footballers. Barrel-chested and a big strong lad, Peter was a powerful, fast defender. Very few opponents got the better of him, but one player Peter hated facing was Terry Paine of Southampton. Terry had a reputation for being able to mix it when necessary and had left his mark against Peter on a number of occasions. Not one to forget, Peter eventually got his revenge at The Dell when Terry almost jumped into the front row to evade him when he came charging in. Off the park, Peter was the perfect gambler. He may have only made a couple of bets a year but he always came up trumps.

Liam O'Kane was a talented and utterly fearless player. We always worried about Liam because he always tackled at full stretch. Our worst fears came to fruition a couple of seasons earlier in a home clash when he broke a leg going for a ball with Everton defender John Hurst. I was on the bench that day and came on as substitute. I went on to the left wing and faced Tommy Wright. After the incident with Liam, the shouts were a case of yours-mine, yours-mine, yours-mine. Nobody was prepared to make a rash tackle and the game petered out but we scraped home 1–0. Liam battled back to full fitness and went on to captain Northern Ireland.

Bernard 'John' Winfield, to give him his full title, was another incredibly strong player, but not the swiftest of footballers. One of the funniest sights I saw on a football pitch was when the ball went between John and West Ham's Bobby Moore. Both were around 30 yards from the ball so it was a clear 50–50. As they approached the ball, both suddenly stopped as they thought the other would make it first. In the end, someone else nipped in for the ball. Both smiled about the incident. Partnering Bernard in defence was our resident joker in the camp, Sammy Chapman, who had been a talented inside forward but converted to a centre half at Forest. Sammy proved reliable despite going through a spell when he seemed to make a crucial mistake every game, costing us a goal. He looked a million dollars for the rest of the match. It was frustrating but he came through and proved a terrific stopper.

Dougie Fraser joined from Midland neighbours West Brom. Nobody could miss Dougie as he had a trademark moustache. Of course, lads being lads, they took the mickey out of him. On his birthday, Tommy Gemmell shaved one half of his moustache off while the lads held him down. Dougie, a terrific squad player, eventually accepted the gag in the spirit it was delivered. Tommy Jackson joined as an exchange while Henry Newton went to Everton. Tommy played many times for Northern Ireland and had an amazing second wind. Tommy had the luck of the Irish because he went on to join Manchester United on a free transfer. He was not a regular so it was a terrific move late in his career.

Of all the young kids who came through our crop of apprentices, Alan Buckley was probably, more than anyone, the blue-eyed boy under Tommy Cavanagh and Frank Knight, though Martin O'Neill enjoyed the greatest success in the long term at the club. Alan had natural talent as a player and was a consummate goal scorer. His height and pace probably stopped him making it at the highest level but he made an impact at Birmingham City and Walsall. Towards the end of his career, I indirectly played a role in Alan joining Division 3 side Walsall as player-manager. When the opportunity arose, Alan rang me for some advice. He said, 'Youth, [I was just younger than him and he never let me forget it] I want a word with you. I'm in Division 1 with Birmingham, why would I want to join Walsall?'

I said, 'Alan, you'll have two jobs. You want to carry on playing but that won't last much longer at the highest level. In Division 3, you can prolong your playing career and try your hand at management. If the management side doesn't work out then you can stop on as a player until something else comes up because they won't sack you as a player.'

Alan said, 'Youth, never thought about that', and took the job. He went on to carve out a successful career as a boss in the lower leagues for years. I'm still waiting for my cut!

John Galley, Neil Martin and George Lyall made their mark in different ways. While John used his height effectively as a target man, Martin, although a centre forward, was a natural leader in the team. Neil always had plenty to say on and off the park about our organisation, how we were performing and so on. Neil was also a big help to me when I made the first team and was always encouraging. He'd constantly scream at me, 'Go on son, take 'em on, have a go, don't be frightened, get past him!' At the time, it was just what I needed to build my confidence. George was a solid, squat midfield player from Preston North End. A reliable penalty taker, George never really got the praise that his creative play deserved.

Paul Richardson was a great man-marker in the team. Nicknamed Linus by the lads after the Charlie Brown comic strip character, Paul stuck to his opponent like glue. I remember in particular Alan Ball being none too happy in one clash when Paul followed his every track. It seemed that Barry Lyons had been at Forest forever. Barry was a world-beater on the five-a-side pitch but never quite produced the goods in first team games. I made my debut when Barry fell ill before a clash at Sunderland. Martin O'Neill was coming into his own as a dangerous player and John Robertson was, for me, the most underrated player at the club. On the wing, John was unstoppable and continued to be a match winner on many occasions.

Dave had incredible trust in the lads and, having been on the fringes for what seemed an eternity, I was ready to make a big impression. Confidence is everything to a footballer and it helps when a manager makes it clear that a player is in his first team line-up. Everyone had defined roles and mine was to go out and cause damage. And if that meant entertaining and making my opponent look stupid at the same time, then so be it.

Dave encouraged me to try things. He'd say to me, push the ball through opponents' legs or he'd tell me to trick my way past opponents. Dave was a winner but also loved showboating. He wanted me to turn it on for both the team and fans because that was his way of playing football. There were things that I did on a pitch that were quite outrageous and at times I surprised myself with what I could achieve by sheer effrontery. I'd almost dare two defenders that had me boxed in a corner to come and take the ball off me. Suddenly, I'd put a seed of doubt in their mind because they'd see how confident I was in my ability to get out of a situation with a bit of trickery. There were occasions when an opponent decided to jockey me and not allow me to make him look a fool.

My newfound attitude helped me start the season on fire. After scoring on the opening day in a 4–0 win over Luton Town, braces followed in victories over Sheffield Wednesday, Swindon Town and Millwall. Nine goals in the opening 10 matches had the football gossip writers taking note. I was on target again in wins over Crystal Palace and Carlisle United, as Forest looked good for a promotion charge.

Life was great and I felt part of the first team set up. The banter was terrific and on long arduous coach journeys I had joined the small card school with Barry Lyons, Jim Barron and Sammy Chapman playing Hearts. We put in around a £1 a hand. These were the days before the motorway network really kicked in so the card games made the journey more bearable. There was no Sky TV, DVDs and iPods, so it was a case of Hearts all the way. On returning home if I had won the card game then Dot and I could splash out on a nice supper, such were the financial restrictions at the time.

Our improved form not only brought me favourable headlines but Dave Mackay was seen as the best young manager around. Derby County clearly had taken note and when the board fell out with Brian Clough and Peter Taylor, Forest turned to Dave after Bobby Robson decided to stay at Ipswich Town. I was disappointed, as Dave had given me my big break. He saw a spark but I realised that he could not miss the challenge of managing his former club even though he had to overcome a players' revolt initially over the decision to fire Cloughie.

Dave Mackay was the key manager in getting me to reach my potential as a footballer and I have always been grateful for that. All the lads respected Dave and he inspired them. Making the grade was tough. Clubs had an inordinate number of apprentices and a manager seldom saw the reserves play competitively as we often played at the same time as the first team. Youngsters had to impress the reserve team coach and with the best will in the world, those responsible for the A team and reserve side often had a different opinion and agenda to the boss. They had blue-eyed boys and not every player got their just reward. Making it in the professional game often comes down to being in the right place at the right time. A manager can give his opinion of what he wants but it does not always follow that his assistants feel the same or see what the manager wants. Having mental toughness is a key factor and fortunately I had plenty.

In my early days at Forest, I had to stand up for myself. Frank Knight and Tommy Cavanaugh were in charge but my face did not fit. Their thinking of playing football was not the same as Johnny Carey, who ran the first team at the time. I remember once getting so frustrated I asked Johnny why I was not in the reserves. I'd scored a hat-trick for the A team but next game I'd still be in the A team. Johnny told me he was at the next A team game, he wanted me to go out and do my own thing. I was not to worry about losing possession, which had been a complaint from Tommy and Frank. Come the game, I waltzed past a couple of defenders and scored. To cap a great game, I also made a goal. Johnny put me in the reserve side meaning I had a small break but you cannot go running to the boss all the time. It was a risky strategy but if you are good enough then you will make it.

Dave was a wonderful motivator and kick-started my career but that comes down to a player's luck. There were players at the club who knew I could play and appealed to previous managers to give me a run, but it was not until Dave arrived that I had the chance. Before Dave, I could have quite easily been down the road because of a lack of opportunities, but I believed that I had talent and was determined to make sure it came through. As a young kid trying to make it, waiting to break through was frustrating and plenty of other hopefuls drifted away from the game.

Many of my problems stemmed from the fact that I'd not

served a full apprenticeship. Other lads came through the ranks. I arrived after others were dropped. There were many so-called experts on Duncan McKenzie telling me what I should and should not do but I am what I am and in time, I'd discover that I was not the only so-called maverick on the park. Nobody was more delighted than I was to be classed alongside Stan Bowles, Frank Worthington, Alan Hudson and Tony Currie. All were showmen in an era when top clubs played 'method' football. Bowles, Worthington, Hudson and Currie ended up at unfashionable clubs QPR, Leicester City, Chelsea and Sheffield United. These football mavericks failed to rack up major honours, but provided rich entertainment which football supporters still appreciate.

Following Dave's departure, Bill Anderson took up the strain as caretaker manager once again until the appointment of Allan Brown who had taken Bury to the fringes of the Division 3 promotion race. Forest continued to stay on the edge of promotion in Division 2 but ultimately finished seventh. The league campaign could not have finished better for me as I scored in our final five fixtures against Carlisle, Bristol City, Cardiff City, Aston Villa and Portsmouth. It is amazing how clubs' fortunes go back and forth. All those sides experienced highs and lows in the intervening years but hit the crest of a wave with fine 2007–08 seasons.

My 26 league goals caused pundits to ask where Duncan McKenzie had been all these years. It was amazing; I'd been knocking on the door for years yet came through with aplomb. In football you never know what is around the corner. Being part of the razzmatazz of the FA Cup for the first time really helped build my profile as Forest enjoyed a fine run in the full glare of the media spotlight. We reached the sixth round for the first time since 1967, which was bizarre because that was the year I'd joined the club. As cup fever gripped Nottingham Forest, I was delighted to play a part in a number of high profile cup games.

Our third round match saw us take on Bristol Rovers, not a big game in normal circumstances. The match was noteworthy for all stattos as it took place on a Sunday, the first ever Sunday match in the competition. And the match was a classic as we came from 2–0 down to win 4–3. The next round pitched us against Manchester City, again on a Sunday, and many Forest fans still say it was the best game they ever saw an individual play at the City Ground. City had many of their big hitters on display including Francis Lee, Colin Bell, Mike Summerbee and Rodney Marsh, though Denis Law did not play. City had class players throughout the side. I faced Mike Doyle and Willie Donachie, notched one goal and made three as Forest won 4–1. I enjoyed one of those games you can only dream about as a player.

Over 41,000 fans packed the City Ground along with what seemed like the whole of Fleet Street to report on a clash dubbed one of the ties in the round. One local journalist noted next day that churchgoers came out saying, 'Be prepared to meet thy God' but instead had the next best thing in Duncan McKenzie. His words were extremely flattering, somewhat embarrassing but most welcome for this young upstart from Grimsby. Forest legend John Robertson still jokes when I see him that Forest won the European Cup twice, but supporters still go on about McKenzie against Manchester City in 1974! John broke into the side that season along with Tony Woodcock and former Manchester City star Ian Bowyer. Alongside Martin O'Neill the quartet would serve Forest with distinction during the glory days to come under Cloughie.

The romance of the FA Cup was alive in the 1970s, unlike in the modern era, until 2007–08 when Barnsley reignited memories of days gone by with victories over Liverpool and Chelsea as they reached the semi-finals. All footballers wanted to play in an FA Cup final at Wembley and I was no different. In the fifth round, I proved to be the hero with a penalty to oust Portsmouth before we faced Newcastle United at a packed St James Park for a much-anticipated quarter-final clash. Unfortunately crowd trouble late on meant the match was abandoned. We led 3–1 with around 15 minutes remaining when Newcastle fans invaded the pitch. It was chaos. The referee ordered the players off the pitch for safety reasons. When we returned to the pitch, the momentum returned to Newcastle who scored three goals to win 4–3. The noise generated from the Toon Army was astonishing as we capitulated. In the dressing room we were distraught as Newcastle's winning goal was clearly offside, a fact vindicated next day on television.

The pitch invasion, in the end, came to Newcastle's rescue as the Football Association ordered the match to be replayed at Goodison Park. Initially we felt aggrieved as the invasion changed the course of the game. There was an argument that Newcastle should have been kicked out of the tournament or, at the very least, the game should have taken place at the City Ground, but we had to get on with it. The clash gave me another chance to impress the masses on television. Unlike today when every big game is covered live, this was a rare opportunity for us to be in the shop window twice in a short period, albeit on a highlights show. I was used to giving local radio and television interviews and so felt comfortable with the media. The build up gave me a chance to be in the spotlight. Journalists dubbed the match the 'Battle of the SuperMacs' with Malcolm Macdonald and me leading the line.

I loved the extra media interest associated with a big cup clash. It was so different to a league game. I was under pressure due to the paper-talk, yet knew this game provided a big chance for me to shine. I could not wait to play but at kick off I was a bag of nerves and froze. I failed to perform. There were no trademark flicks or tricks and we held our own in a 0–0 draw. The match went to a second replay, which we lost to a Macdonald goal. It was a massive disappointment after all the hype. Newcastle made it to Wembley before freezing as Liverpool outclassed them. For some time I felt hard done by due to the pitch invasion, but the publicity surrounding the replay taught me a valuable lesson. I'd been built up to be a superstar too quickly. Confidence is great but you have to be able to handle the big stage and I knew I'd be better prepared next time.

By the end of the campaign, I'd struck 28 goals in all competitions, which was terrific. I'd played 49 matches throughout the season and my consistent scoring resulted in rumours that top clubs were interested in signing me. I did not particularly want to leave Nottingham Forest because I'd finally cracked it and made the first team. On the other hand, playing top flight football was the only thing I wanted to do. To read that suitors included Everton appealed to me due to my family connections on Merseyside. Plaudits had been plenty and I was especially delighted to gain recognition by peers in the PFA Division 2 XI.

When analysing the list of names in the team, we could have given any Division 1 side a run for its money. The full line-up was some team as it comprised Bryan King (Millwall), John Craggs (Middlesbrough), Dave Watson (Sunderland), Willie Madden (Middlesbrough), John Gorman (Carlisle United), Bruce Rioch (Derby County), Don Masson (Notts County), Asa Hartford (West Brom), Dennis Tueart (Sunderland), Duncan

McKenzie (Nottingham Forest) and Don Rogers (Crystal Palace).

The nominated side had a great character in goalkeeper Bryan King. John Craggs was a dependable defender while Dave Watson was clearly a star in the making at centre half (as he'd prove in years to come for Manchester City and England). Willie Madden partnered him and always performed solidly. John Gorman made the team alongside Bruce Rioch, who went on to excel at Everton and Scotland. Don Masson went on skipper QPR and Scotland while another Scot in the side was Asa Hartford. At the time he was still at the Baggies after his dream move to Leeds United collapsed following medical reports that revealed a hole in the heart. Asa made a mockery of that diagnosis for years to come as a wonderful left-sided midfielder with Manchester City and Scotland.

In attack, Dennis Tueart was a dangerous opponent and backed his own ability with a stack of goals. I lined up alongside Don Rogers who made his name at Swindon Town prior to making this line-up. Out of this particular XI, a number of future stars would go on to prove their ability at the highest level. Without being disrespectful it wouldn't be possible to name a similar team of such standing from the modern second tier of English football. Not every player in the team could be viewed a top flight player of the future but Watson, Rioch, Masson, Hartford, Tueart and Rogers were class acts.

Away from fantasy football, Division 1 outfits were not the only ones to notice my performances because incredibly Sir Alf Ramsey had selected me for the England squad in the end of season Home International championships. These were the days when England faced Scotland, Wales and Northern Ireland annually but with increased problems with rival fans, especially when England played Scotland, and a growing trend to have far more qualification games in European and World Cup tournaments, the Home Internationals would disappear from the mainstream fixture list. The competition's demise was a shame as the England versus Scotland clash in particular was a showpiece event and the only guaranteed live match outside the FA Cup final at Wembley each season.

Harold Alcock was on the Nottingham Forest committee and had a say in which players broke into the England squad. Harold put my name forward as a player with potential. Alf called me up for a friendly match in April 1974 against Portugal in Lisbon and I was only a hairsbreadth from making my international debut before fate stepped in. I was selected as the only forward on the bench and when Malcolm Macdonald pulled a muscle in the first half I thought, 'This is my chance.'

But Alf turned around and in his distinctive voice said, 'I'm frightfully sorry Duncan but we're having a bit of a rough ride. I need to shore things up.' Looking at Bally (Alan Ball), he told him to get stripped. Alf put Bally into the middle to make it five across midfield. England drew the match 0–0.

Of course, I was disappointed because for just a brief moment I thought, 'This is it for the kid from Grimsby.' Playing for your country is every schoolboy's dream, but it was not to be.

I felt let down to get so close but this was my first trip with the full international squad so I was sure another opportunity would come my way. My England selection cranked up the media speculation and helped raise the stakes about my current playing contract that was due for negotiation during the close season. The summer months in 1974 would be among the most stressful I'd face as a professional footballer as my future came under the spotlight.

4

TRANSFER SHENANIGANS AND LIFE WITH CLOUGHIE

As the 1974–75 season approached, my future was in the melting pot. I had been the subject of much media speculation but ideally wanted to stay at Nottingham Forest so long as the club remunerated me fairly. After a meeting with manager Allan Brown to discuss my contract, I told local journalists I was happy to commit my immediate future to the club. The decision went down well with Forest supporters as they saw me as central to rebuilding a promotion-chasing team.

Forest wanted all the good publicity they could get to generate a feel-good factor for the new season and news that I'd agreed, in principle, a new contract no doubt helped season ticket sales. But all my plans were thrown into chaos when I saw the fine detail of the terms. My wage was nowhere near what I expected the going rate to be for a player of my standing. I felt bitterly let down by the club. I demanded a meeting to clear the air with chairman Jim Wilmer. A date was set but on the day of the meeting, club officials informed me that both the chairman and manager were on holiday. I was fuming. My Forest future was now in the balance. I rang the manager who bluntly told me to put a transfer request in writing if I was not happy. I refused and threatened to quit football, which meant Forest would not get a transfer fee. The club branded me a rebel but I felt aggrieved at how Forest had reacted after our initial negotiations.

Since joining the club, I'd been loyal but I felt I was on terrible wages. I was contracted at £30 a week, though Forest had paid me £50 for six months, when comparative players were getting £200 a week. We were at an impasse. Eventually, the club contacted me. I duly went along to a meeting attended by both the manager and chairman. We agreed to meet again to finalise terms. Arriving at the ground, I discovered the manager was playing golf. I was flabbergasted. The chairman eventually arrived and after making me wait for some considerable time, he informed me that my wage aspirations could not be agreed.

I'd finished last season as top scorer by some distance, was being talked up in the media and sensed that things were beginning to take off for me. I asked for my cards but the club refused, even though they knew it was illegal as my contract was up. At home it was also a stressful time as Dot was eight months' pregnant. My protracted problems at Forest were not helping. We had no money and it looked like being a difficult summer. Something had to give but I knew that there was no future for me at the club. Although I'd threatened to quit, both the club and I knew it was just hot-headedness, as I wanted to continue my professional football career.

At Forest, I had been 'Happy as Larry' and bedded into the team, scoring goals galore. Forest had a great set of lads. There were no prima donnas and the camaraderie was fantastic. But the manner in which club officials had treated me was a real kick in the teeth. Derek Dougan, Professional Footballers Association chairman at the time, offered to mediate, but I wanted to sort my

Mum, dad and me circa 1950

In 1952 big Christmas trees were too expensive for the McKenzie household

Playing chess at school

Mum and dad

With nan and granddad

Playing against Manchester City as a youngster in 1974 in a Sunday FA Cup tie. Forest won 4–1

Nottingham Forest, 1973–74 season ©*Press Association*

Scoring a second goal against Brum for Leeds ©*Andrew Varley*

Playing for Leeds with Sir Trevor in the background   *©Andrew Varley*

Taking a shot at goal for Leeds
                    ©Andrew Varley

Playing in the Charity Shield for Leeds: sadly we lost   *©Andrew Varley*

Training with Joe Mercer's England Squad, 1975   *©Press Association*

Leeds v West Ham in 1975

©Andrew Varley

My wife Dot, son Andrew and me enjoying a meal when we first arrived at Anderlecht

The family at home in Anderlecht—we loved the lifestyle!

Training with the squad in Anderlecht

own future out, although I appreciated his call and promised to call back if I needed advice. I stayed away from the club and waited.

When I missed a pre-season training session, for what I believed was a fair reason, as I was in dispute with the club, Bill Anderson pulled up outside our house. Bill got out of his car and tried to make me look a fool in front of my neighbour who was in the front garden. I was livid and told Bill where to go. I would not allow anyone to ridicule me outside my own home. Bill apologised and we went inside where we had a frank discussion. I was disgusted with the way Forest had treated me and told him I'd make no assurances to attend training. Word was soon out that I was on the market and the phone started to ring from interested clubs.

The first to express an interest was Birmingham City boss Freddie Goodwin. He said, 'Duncan, it's Freddie here, I'd like to think we are mates.'

I thought to myself, 'I've only met him once.'

Freddie said, 'Do me a favour, when you go to Manchester United, Liverpool, Leeds United or Tottenham Hotspur, would you tell them that I tried to sign you for Birmingham?' I laughed because I knew where he was coming from. Freddie was just sounding me out with no expectation of me wanting to join his club. He then explained that Birmingham fans felt he had to be in for every big player available but they did not have any money.

Tottenham boss Bill Nicholson then rang and I have to admit, playing for Bill Nich was appealing because of the style of football that he believed in. But London life was not for me. I had the utmost respect for Bill, but with the best will in the world, I did not have a shilling, lived in a very modest house and could not dream of living in London. I was very flattered by his interest though. I promised Bill I'd not go to another London club. There were plenty of rumours linking me to other clubs including Derby County because of Dave Mackay, but there was no chance of me going to the Baseball Ground. Dave wanted me, yet knew he would not be able to do a deal. Dave would have paid the kitchen sink for me. Unfortunately Forest held my registration and would not sell me to Derby of all clubs. It was a closed shop. I could have gone to court because their actions could have been deemed a restraint of trade but my hands were tied as I had no money.

Out of the blue, new Leeds United boss Brian Clough entered the scene. It was a surprise to many that Cloughie had succeeded Don Revie as manager at Elland Road because he'd been unbelievably outspoken against the club for a number of years. Cloughie was a controversial character and one of the game's real personalities. He'd guided Derby to Division 1 and 2 titles before a brief spell at Brighton and Hove Albion ended farcically. Cloughie spoke his mind and the media loved him because he was always ready to give his thoughts, many of which were outrageous. It was common knowledge at the time that Leeds players and supporters had not welcomed his arrival with open arms, but that did not concern me. I had a chance to play for a top manager who I felt could improve my game and I'd be at a club everyone wanted to beat. Competition for places would be fierce but the challenge excited me. Leeds United played to packed crowds home and away. News that Cloughie was interested was music to my ears. This was the club for me.

Leeds and Nottingham Forest agreed a fee of £250,000. I just had to agree terms and that meant negotiating with Cloughie, who was an intimidating individual. I'd met Brian only once before but he did not know me. Our brief meeting came when I was among a group of Nottingham Forest lads who tried to blag our way into the Baseball Ground when he was boss. At the time, I had an old Morris Minor but it was a death trap. The foot brake barely worked, I had to pump it hard to stop the car. The hand brake, on one scary occasion, came off in my hand. MOTs were not as stringent as today but I was only an apprentice so could not afford anything better. More to the point, I was the only ground staff lad with wheels so was resident chauffeur to the lads. We all piled into my car for the short journey to Derby but safety was not uppermost in my mind, as I knew that if we broke down, I wouldn't have to push because I had readymade volunteers! Tongue in cheek and armed only with Forest players' passes, we presented them to club officials. Seconds later Cloughie came out and told us to wait after hearing our request. With a glint in his eye Cloughie duly went off and came back with tickets. He knew we were pulling a fast one but with a wry smile and, in his distinctive voice, told us he hoped he'd be looked after when he next came to the City Ground. Trying to look composed we agreed with his request and thanked the great man.

When Cloughie rang me at home to discuss the biggest move of my life, I was both terrified and thrilled at the same time. He said, 'Duncan, Brian Clough here. Now then Duncan, don't piss me about young man, I have half a chance of signing you. Are you going to that Dave Mackay at Derby County, because I know you've been tapped up, or would you like to sign for me at Leeds United?'

I diplomatically told him I'd love the opportunity of speaking to him and gave assurances I'd not signed for anyone. Cloughie said, 'Good lad, now go pack your bags and meet me at the Victoria Hotel, Sheffield. And don't be late.'

My head was spinning as I tootled down the M1 motorway with Dot and our afghan hound in tow on the back seat of our NSU

2-stroke Prinz car. We arrived at the Victoria Hotel as planned. The first thing in my favour was that we could sense the Leeds' boss was scared stiff of dogs as he walked towards us with a couple of champagne bottles, announcing he'd be with us in a minute as he was in the middle of a meal. Cloughie returned and asked if we had permission to have a hound in the hotel. I said that we had. Reluctantly nodding okay, Cloughie said, 'Now tell me Duncan, how much did you ask Nottingham Forest for?' I told him. He said, 'Right, done, now sign here.' That was it. I was given three blank contracts and signed them feeling a very relieved footballer. I had been skint but now had peace of mind for Dot that I was in gainful employment.

With negotiations concluded, Cloughie asked when the baby was due. He told Dot to have a dose of cod liver oil and get the baby on the move so I could get on with my football. We were both a bit stunned by the advice but knew it was just a typical Cloughie comment. We arranged for Dot's brother, Billy, to pick her up while I followed my new boss to Elland Road in our car. I had no chance of keeping up with Cloughie's top of the range motor, though, and arrived 20 minutes afterwards. Cloughie said, 'You're late, so you have just lost your first week's wages.' I wasn't sure whether to believe him but Cloughie did have a glint in his eye. As it turned out it was just Cloughie being Cloughie. I smiled and of course lost no wages.

When Brian Clough wanted something, he came straight to the point. There was no messing about. Cloughie wanted to sign me, listened to my terms and said okay. Over the years, people have found it difficult to believe that negotiations went so smoothly but that was it. I was delighted it had been so simple and maybe I could have negotiated better terms, but I was not complaining. I was joining a massively experienced squad packed with international players who were household names. I'd signed for the defending league champions in August 1974. I was Cloughie's first signing, finally in big time football and it felt terrific.

At Elland Road, I attended a press conference. Cloughie took centre stage and was in his element. He asked who was representing the *Sunday Mirror*. When the journalist made himself known, Cloughie sent him packing for stitching him up in the previous Sunday's newspaper. Another reporter asked when I'd make my debut. Cloughie was quick with his repost, 'When I chuffing pick him!' This style of questioning continued for the next 20 minutes. A journalist asked a question and Cloughie fired back a reply quick as a flash giving nothing away. Brian was on form and in control. I barely said a word at my own press conference. I went to the Dragonara Hotel to settle into a room until I found a place locally.

When I joined Leeds, I felt like a millionaire. My salary had started at £12 a week and gone up to £50 a week before I joined Leeds. The contract was nothing particularly special as there were no goal bonuses, just a win bonus. As a member of the full England squad I had been earning a quarter of most players' salaries and now suddenly it was a case of rags to riches. I earned in a week what I used to earn in a month at Nottingham Forest. The transfer also meant that I was entitled to five percent of the transfer fee. This totalled £13,333 over a number of payments during a two-year contract. Football finances in the seventies were naive at best. When I got my first pay packet at my new club, I didn't know what to do with it all. I thought, 'To hell with it', and we booked a holiday to New York. I bought a new car for the first time in my life. I decided to have some fun but I didn't want to spend it all.

Looking back at my Forest years, Dave Mackay was the biggest influence, although he was manager for only a short spell.

Dave encouraged me to make a difference on the field to gain an advantage. Opponents could not anticipate my movement so this gave me an edge and Dave wanted to see that reflected in my game. I did not enjoy accentuating the negatives regarding Forest when contract negotiations stalled, but felt pushed into a corner. Allan Brown and Jim Wilmer acted dreadfully. I'd rather they had levelled with fans saying the club needed funds to rebuild. That would have been far better than being cloak and dagger about my transfer. All that was history as I began a new chapter in my footballing career.

Joining Leeds United, I'd soon be playing with star internationals such as Billy Bremner, Norman Hunter, Johnny Giles, Peter Lorimer, Paul Madeley and Eddie Gray. Young players who had come through the ranks like Joe Jordan and Terry Yorath were also full internationals. Trevor Cherry, who arrived from Huddersfield Town a couple of years earlier, and Allan Clarke from Leicester City, were the only other big-money transfers from the Don Revie era. I was excited at the prospect of playing with all this talent. Leeds had won every domestic honour and gone close on many other occasions. They were an ageing side but still very talented and the big target for the season was the European Cup, a trophy that had eluded them. Although they were defending Division 1 champions, I didn't feel intimidated because I was a cocky little bugger and was confident I'd impress my new teammates.

After the first training session Cloughie came into the dressing room and saw me smoking. He said, 'Hey Smokey Joe, pack them fags in or get yourself another club.'

I joked, 'Five percent, where am I going?'

Cloughie said, 'Very funny', and walked away but not before telling me I'd be making my debut in the first ever Charity Shield at Wembley against FA Cup holders Liverpool. I'd be on the bench.

I asked whether there was a chance of any complimentary tickets for my parents. Cloughie snapped back in his inimitable style, 'If your parents won't pay to see you play, why would any other bugger do so?'

I took that as a no but received some tickets anyway. It was just Cloughie being Cloughie and not letting me get above my station.

The early training sessions I took part in as I settled into the team were a real football education. As a player, you have to think you're the best. You must have belief in your own ability. I had bundles of ability but it was only when I saw star players around me at close quarters that I realised just how good they really were. Lining up for the five-a-sides and shooting practice were Lorimer, Clarke, Bremner, Giles, Hunter and so on, all class acts known throughout the football world. There were plenty of cracks from the lads, especially from Billy. As I walked into the changing room carrying my kit bag, he'd shout, 'Got your signing on fee in the bag Duncan?' And there were plenty of other pranksters ready to strike.

Wembley was renowned as a magical stadium for atmosphere. It was ranked alongside stadia such as Old Trafford, Anfield, the Nou Camp and Parc des Princes Stadium. But playing at Wembley was what all footballers dream of. Consequently, I was really looking forward to my first game for Leeds as it was my first appearance at the Twin Towers. The game ended in disappointment as we lost to Liverpool on penalties. The clash was a poor game riddled with some tasty fouls from both teams. It was anything but a pre-season friendly. In the end, the game was infamous for a scrap between Bremner and Kevin Keegan that resulted in both being sent off. Phil Boersma opened the scoring for Liverpool, Trevor Cherry equalised for Leeds, but we lost 6–5 in the shoot-out when David Harvey blazed over. I got a run out and was well received by the Leeds contingent in the stands.

Much as I knew that there would be no favouritism from Cloughie, I was still taken aback when he came on the pitch at full time and, pointing at me, told the lads I would not be taking a penalty. I was not going to argue but felt miffed. Back in the dressing room, I mentioned it to him but he didn't want a situation where I missed and possibly got the fans against me straight away. I pointed out that I might have scored the winner but it was all too late.

Before the opening league game of the season we played in a testimonial match for Ted Bates at The Dell, Southampton. We flew down from Leeds-Bradford Airport, had lunch when we arrived, played the game and flew back. I was fast asleep back at the Dragonara in the early hours when my room phone went. A voice said 'Duncan, Brian Clough here. Reception five minutes and don't be late.' I could not quite believe it and wondered what was wrong.

I freshened up and raced to reception. Sitting down at a table, I asked if there was a problem.

Cloughie said 'Yes, don't let me see you get off a plane in that condition again.'

I said, 'What condition? Sober?'

After defending myself a couple of times that I had not had a drink and in fact did not drink, Cloughie said, pointing at a glass, 'You will be soon', and then with a wry smile, asked whether I wanted tea or coffee. At that moment I realised Brian Clough was a lonely man and wanted company, particularly because of the situation he was in at Elland Road. I was aware of infighting when he got the post and suddenly it clicked. As the new kid on the block, I had no history with the Revie players so he felt comfortable with me.

Tongue in cheek, Cloughie noted while we were having coffee that I had enjoyed lunch with a number of the lads. Cloughie wanted to know what they had said about him. I said the players had not mentioned him and made it clear that if we had talked about him, then he would not find out about it from me. Cloughie said he'd paid a quarter of a million pounds for my services and wanted my support. I said that he'd get my full support in every way, but I would not tell tales. He respected my views, we chatted for a while and then I went back to my room feeling sorry for my club manager.

Come the opening league game, with Allan Clarke suspended and Mick Jones injured (Mick would be forced to retire), I made my full debut in an opening day 3–0 defeat to Stoke City. Nothing went right from the kick off and, during the game, an exasperated Cloughie ran to the sidelines and yelled at me in his inimitable style, 'Young man, I pay you to score goals and you won't score any in our half. Get on that halfway line and do what I paid all that money for.' I did this but it made no difference on the day. Afterwards he had a quiet word and made it clear that when I was in the team, I had to be in the danger zone. I noted that I wanted to do my share of checking back but staying in attack was fine by me. Cloughie wanted me to be myself. I was determined to make an impression and play my own game in our next clash at home to Queens Park Rangers but picked up an injury. To make matters worse, we suffered another defeat. Cloughie was sacked a couple of days after I played a reserve match to test my fitness.

I only played a short time for Brian Clough but his appointment, looking back, was a disaster waiting to happen. Even though Cloughie made a massive impact on me as a footballer and person, Revie and Clough's thinking were poles apart. Brian criticised Leeds' tactics in the media and this was not well received, unsurprisingly, in Yorkshire. The two of them were at each other's throats in the press. Cloughie tried to change things far too quickly but Leeds United and Clough was a marriage doomed to fail and Clough's appointment was a dreadful decision by the directors.

Shortly after departing Leeds, Brian rang me and was his total domineering self on the phone. 'Young man,' he said, 'Queens Hotel, 30 minutes. And don't be late.' I wasn't even playing for Cloughie but I still went because he had that effect on players.

He said, 'Young man, I'll mark your card. All your nutmegs, flicks, back heels and tricks, never change them because that is what the punters love and it's been successful for you. It's made you the player that you are and it's why I signed you for Leeds United.' Listening to his comments, his views were most welcome. Cloughie would try to sign me a couple more times in the coming years, when he joined Nottingham Forest as manger and when I signed for Everton, but neither club would do business. Although our paths never crossed professionally again, he rated me as a player and that has always meant a lot to me.

From time to time I bumped into Brian after my playing career was over on corporate visits to Nottingham Forest. Every time I saw him, he always found time for a quick chat and even paid me an unexpected visit one Christmas. I was in the bath when my son, Andrew, ran upstairs shouting that Brian Clough and the Forest team were at the front door singing carols. Jokingly I told him to give them 50p and tell them to go away. But Andrew said he was not joking and it was indeed a pleasant surprise when I went downstairs. Chatting to the lads, my former teammate John Robertson told me he was responsible for giving away our address. I thought to myself, 'Thanks John, I owe you one.'

After a quick toast and cursory nod of affection by Cloughie, he yelled, 'Right lads!' and off they went.

Brian remained a real character throughout his managerial career. Through former referee, Neil Midgley, God bless him, I was able to see my former club play occasionally. Neil always had a tale afterwards because you could rely on Cloughie to be on great form. In one particular clash, just before half time, Kenny Burns whacked Mark Falco for a clear penalty and Spurs scored. Waiting for the players to return for the second half, Cloughie put a welcoming arm around Neil's chest. 'A quick word about the penalty,' Cloughie said. 'Burns hit Falco, no doubt about it. He'll be disciplined for that as it was a bad foul but,' with a wry smile, 'was it in the penalty area?'

Neil explained that the linesman, who was better placed to judge it, had signalled an infringement and it was in the area. Cloughie winked, 'I'm sure you'll have a better view of incidents in the second half Neil', and ran off in his green sweatshirt down the tunnel. Neil laughed. Officials respected Cloughie because they knew exactly where they stood.

Although many aspects of the game have improved over time, one area where there was more respect was in terms of communicating with officials. Of course, there were incidents and fans gave refs a hard time, but I barely remember referees being berated by players or managers in the way they are today. There was better man-management from officials during games. Players just got on with it. Refs would come in before a game and spell out what they expected. Harold Hackney would say, 'Gentlemen the game is football. Don't raise a hand to opponents and no bad language in my direction. Enjoy the game.' And then there were the likes of Roger Fitzpatrick who would run up and down with his knees pumping high in the air. By his own admission, his style of running diffused a difficult situation because he was a character with both players and fans alike. Fans would laugh but in a nice way. The players also had tremendous respect for the likes of Gordon Hill, Pat Partridge and Jack Taylor. All were class referees as they understood the game and used common sense to make tough decisions.

In my view, modern day referees are not as good. They don't seem focused enough on the job in hand but it's not all their fault. There is far too much surrounding the role in terms of pleasing assessors, fourth officials and coaches. There is too much on a referee's plate. The game survived for over a century before the world of assessors and the like, but I accept the spectre of television replays hangs over decisions like never before. Spats with managers were almost non-existent, but now players and managers are in the ref and fourth official's faces at every decision. Professionalising the role with jobs for the boys has been detrimental to the overall effect a referee has on a game.

Over the years, much has been written about Brian Clough's 44-day stay at Leeds United and of course, it has been documented in the film *The Damned United*. Opinions are varied but it depends on whether you were an outsider to events at Elland Road or a Revie old boy as to where you stand. In hindsight, the appointment was doomed to fail, as there was so much bad feeling between Cloughie and the club. Because Brian had criticised Revie and the players down the years, it was an impossible task. And it was not a question of one criticising and the other not saying anything, the two were never short in giving their two-penneth of views. During my brief period at the club while Cloughie was manager, it was palpable during team meetings when he made a point that Syd Owen would be mumbling under his breath close by, disagreeing with everything. The atmosphere was not great and it was clear to me that Brian could hear Syd. He ignored the mumblings to avoid confrontation while he was trying to settle in, but it was apparent discontent was simmering.

The Leeds board made a major error of judgement. They could have attracted any manager in the land, but got it wrong big time and it cost them a small fortune in compensation. Cloughie told me when the dust had settled that his pay off was a nest egg and had set him up for life. Brian's stay was all so brief but, that said, there were inherent problems in the Leeds camp that I sensed on my arrival. It is well documented Revie recommended Giles as his successor but Bremner also wanted to be manager and had his allies. Wanting to avoid conflict, the United board went for Clough. Johnny proved his talents as a manager at West Brom while Billy enjoyed success at Doncaster Rovers and briefly at Leeds while they were a Division 2 outfit, but expectations from supporters and the media were vastly different from being among favourites for honours.

It's now pure conjecture, but if the Leeds board had stayed stronger and refused to sack Brian, a few years down the line, when the Revie team had broken up, it may have worked out. Papers talked about player power but in the end, the chairman had to make a decision, which meant I'd be playing for a new manager. But I was not the only Cloughie signing as John McGovern and John O'Hare had also joined. Both had been successful at Derby when they won the league title in 1972 under Cloughie, but neither had an opportunity to shine as Brian was shown the door. McGovern went on to star at Forest under his former mercurial boss.

Since retiring, one of the questions I am always asked on the after-dinner circuit, is what it was like playing for Brian Clough. The honest answer is that it's impossible to say, as I didn't play for him that long. Brian was some character. I saw the antics, heard all the one-liners and felt inspired by his comments. Having known Cloughie, I can't help but wonder how the current media pack would have handled him. For certain the WAGs would have got short shrift and players would have known where they stood. History shows that Brian became one of the great post-war managers. Fans loved or hated him but no one can knock his record. Winning two European Cups with a provincial club puts him up there with the very best, and domestically he was one of the greats. Cloughie was undoubtedly the best manager overlooked by England. Brian should have been made England manager when Don Revie left the post in 1977 and who knows, I may have got that elusive England cap.

People also ask me whether I had a rough ride, in the early days in particular, from the Leeds lads. Yes I did, but new players, especially a club record signing, always have to show their worth. I knew the score. I'd signed for a massive fee and had to impress. Glances at first were sideways. I was new and here was a group of lads who had been together for years. It was obvious that some of them were coming to the end of careers at a club they had graced with distinction, but there was a reluctance to break up the Revie team. I was clearly a threat.

I was not perceived to be a team player and also had the dubious honour of being the first player to join after Revie. All I could do was knuckle down. In fairness to supporters, from day one the Leeds faithful gave me great support. We had an instant rapport and it is still present when I go back to the club. Teammates would not treat me like somebody special, and rightly so, as I had to prove my worth. The only way to do that is to play, score goals and contribute to the team performance. I knew there were flaws to my game, but I was more determined than ever to succeed.

As for the film *The Damned United*, which is based on the

book, the Clough family is disappointed by the novel but I found it remarkably close to the truth. The film has in a number of errors in to turn it back into a novel and to me it was more a portrayal of the Clough/Taylor relationship than the 44 days at Elland Road. I thought it was quite amusing to see Johnny Giles at 6ft 3in and I was a tad disappointed not to be played by Brad Pitt but when it turned out to be Joseph Dempsie I could understand the difference in vocabulary. But if you blinked you'd miss my line. Overall though, all the characters are well acted and I thought it was a reasonable and believable portrayal of events.

5

LIFE AFTER CLOUGHIE AND EUROPEAN HEARTACHE

When I joined Leeds United, nobody would have received odds from a bookmaker on me playing for three managers by Christmas 1974. That was the reality of the situation as the board considered whom to appoint. Initially, Maurice Lindley took over as caretaker manager, backed up by Tony Collins and Syd Owen. I got on well with Lindley and found Collins the most personable, but Owen was bitter and twisted in his bias towards the Revie lads. I understood Syd's loyalty, yet times were changing at the club and everyone connected with Revie needed to accept he was no longer presiding over events at Elland Road.

Internally the club was a mess and I was in the middle of sentimental Revie balderdash, which was extremely frustrating. No club can rest on its laurels, it has to move forward, but at the time Leeds United seemed incapable of doing so. Lindley wanted to calm things down until a new manager arrived and, encouraged by Collins, did not want to subject me to the abuse that John O'Hare and John McGovern received as ex-Cloughie players when they made debuts in a scratchy win over

Birmingham City. Luckily we had matches coming up thick and fast.

The big target for the club was the European Cup. It was the one trophy to escape Revie's aces and they knew that this was a last crack at winning the ultimate European trophy. The lads would put everything into it and when the first round came along, I was fit again. Lindley put me on the bench for an opening round clash with FC Zurich. We won comfortably 5–2 on aggregate. I was not required for either leg so Lindley gave me a run out against Huddersfield Town in a League Cup replay that ended in a 1–1 draw.

By the European Cup second round, Jimmy Armfield was manager and his appointment was not before time. Jimmy had managed Bolton Wanderers to promotion in his first managerial post after a distinguished playing career with Blackpool and England. On and off the pitch, the club was in turmoil when Jimmy took the helm. Leeds needed a strong boss to sort out things. Cloughie had the required attributes but there was too much history. Brian blazed a trail with unpopular decisions that got players backs up whereas Jimmy immediately settled things down with his approach to management.

Unassuming, diplomatic and approachable, Jimmy was calmness personified whereas Cloughie was a control-freak and born winner. Jimmy's demeanour was more that of a bank manager rather than a football manager and for three decades it has puzzled me why he went into management at all. I think Jimmy just loved the game and wanted to stay involved. Back in late 1974, Jimmy had the toughest ask in football, as he had to break up a side packed with strong characters and world class footballers while attempting to compete for major honours. An Armfield team talk was considered and the lads quickly dubbed him Gentleman Jim. We had a standing joke that the manager's indecision was final. Okay, it was cruel but Jimmy did pontificate. Watching training from the sidelines, Jim would puff on his pipe and deliberate for some time before saying a word.

Leeds United were the most feared club side in England. After gaining promotion in 1964, the team had gained an unwanted reputation that saw them labelled 'Dirty Leeds' by the media. I played against the great side when Bremner, Charlton, Giles, Hunter and co. were in their pomp. They were hard, but never dirty and there is a difference. Leeds were the ultimate professional outfit and for me, the best club team English football has produced and ranked alongside the legendary Real Madrid team that included Di Stefano and Puskas. Arguments will always rage about which club is the best and you can only compare like with like in an era. Back in the late sixties and early seventies, Leeds had a wonderful team. Tottenham Hotspur striker Jimmy Greaves used to say that if you played Leeds at football, they'd murder you and if you fought them, they'd still murder you. Revie's Leeds had everything.

Leeds played some of the greatest football witnessed in the late sixties and early seventies. There was pace, power and style, yet I never saw wondrous tactics or special moves in training. Leeds had star players who could improvise. Revie and his team have their place in history. Supporters treat the star players as heroes and historians recognise the team's achievements. Outside Leeds, though, opposing supporters hated them and the media only gave grudging acceptance as to how good they actually were. The club was loathed rather than loved but when on song they were unbeatable. What I find gratifying is that on the after-dinner circuit, former players from other clubs acknowledge the greatness of the side. Led by Bremner, Leeds United in their pomp could battle and entertain to equal effect.

Unfortunately Revie left a legacy that future managers have

found impossible to follow. Even Howard Wilkinson, who led the side to a third league crown, has never been truly appreciated. What Wilko did with Gordon Strachan leading the side was amazing during the early nineties as Leeds won two divisional titles in three seasons. As a team under Revie, Leeds, however successful, did not achieve all they should have done. Leeds United won major honours but finished runners-up on far too many occasions. I'd discover that scenario from the sidelines in the European Cup final in months to come. One can only speculate why the Leeds lads failed at the last gasp but three decades on, time has not diminished the greatness of Revie's side.

For me, joining this great club was a challenge and breaking into the team was tough. The side had grown up as a unit and played as a unit. Jimmy Armfield was a calming influence and made me feel very much a part of his squad. And he gave me a huge boost of confidence by selecting me to play against Arsenal in his first match at the helm. In some ways I was fortunate as Jimmy had seen me play for Nottingham Forest at Burnden Park the previous season and I had clearly impressed him. Before the game against the Gunners, Jimmy told me to play like the young devil that rang rings around his Bolton team in a 3–2 win at the City Ground. I'd also shone when Bolton sneaked a win at Burnden Park. Jimmy believed I could perform at the highest level. I wanted to prove him right.

Leeds defeated the Gunners with a brace by yours truly in a 2–0 victory but that did not stop Johnny Giles rollicking me after going on a solo run looking for a hat-trick. John felt I should have played a simple pass as I could have lost possession and handed the advantage to Arsenal. I understood what Johnny was saying but that was not my game. I played off the cuff. I realised that it could be a problem because the Revie lads were not going to change their style so I'd have to fit in. Flicks and spontaneous tricks proved successful at Forest but I did lose possession if a teammate failed to read my game. Leeds had built a reputation for playing method football in the main, so I was a bit of a culture shock, but I was not down for long as Leeds fans chanted 'Duncan McKenzie is magic' from the terraces.

It was great to be on song and I enjoyed a run in the side. Another goal came my way to secure a 2–0 win over Wolves and Jimmy kept faith with me for a first leg clash at Hungarian giants, Ujpest Dozsa. I was really looking forward to my European debut in Budapest, but it was a disaster as I was sent off inside 15 minutes. From the first whistle, centre half Josef Horvath was allowed to hack me. German referee Kurt Tschenscher stood and smiled each time I got battered. I've never been so beaten up in my life. I was involved in a move that saw Lorimer give us an early lead before a moment of madness ruined my European bow.

During an attack, Horvath hacked me down from behind. Instinctively I retaliated. I jumped up and stamped on him. Obviously, it was a heat of the moment reaction and was a stupid thing to do. I rightly received my marching orders. I'd been done and realised it instantly. I deeply regretted my reaction because I'd let both my teammates and myself down. Jimmy, cool as you like, was puffing away on his pipe. He looked at me as if to say, a bit silly that Duncan. I thought to myself as I seethed away that it wasn't him getting kicked to Kingdom Come. But I'd been naive. It would prove to be my one and only match in Europe for the club. The lads showed European mettle to pull off a 2–1 victory before wrapping up a 5–1 aggregate win at home.

With Lorimer, Jordan and Giles injured for short periods, I remained in the side over the New Year period and developed a growing rapport with the Leeds fans. Goals were also coming my way, which was a bonus. A brace earned a draw with Middlesbrough while other efforts brought victories over Carlisle United and Tottenham Hotspur. The festive period in particular brought success as I scored in successive league wins over Leicester, West Ham and Chelsea. My strike at Leicester was particularly pleasing. When the ball came to me, I had a split second to weigh up my options. I decided to drag the ball back away from a defender before chipping into the far corner of the net. The goal was captured on one of three televised games on *Match of the Day*. These were the days when not every game was on the Saturday night must-watch show. It earned third spot in the Goal of the Season competition. I was delighted. Another strike sealed a 4–1 win over Cardiff City in the FA Cup.

Off the pitch, I'd settled down and was roped into a starring role in Norman Hunter's testimonial pantomime. Norman benefited from my willingness to get involved after persuading me to take on the role of Cinders in the Christmas Pantomime as part of a fundraiser. On a night of rich entertainment with all the lads involved, the punch lines came thick and fast. 'Here comes Cinders straight from the Forest', 'Rags to Riches', and so on. It was tremendous fun but it was only after arriving home that I realised why I'd received strange looks when filling up at a petrol station. I still had my Cinders make up on!

Life was fine and dandy when suddenly goals started to dry up, which happens to all footballers. It was something that I just had to work through until it came right. From my perspective, I was still the newcomer and vying for a place alongside Clarke, Jordan and Lorimer. One of us invariably had to miss out. With the modern rotation system, it would have been easy, but in the seventies, managers played what they considered a first XI bar injury or suspension. Injuries gave me a run, but to his credit Jimmy did play Allan in a deeper role to accommodate me when

Joe was fit and also switched Peter to midfield. Aside from tactical issues, there was an indirect pressure to play me, as it was a problem having the club's most expensive player on the bench. But I had to deliver.

Switching positions was an occupational hazard for some footballers but others were able to build their reputation on the back of it. It worked for Paul Madeley in what seemed any position while Frank Gray moved from midfield to become a world class left back. Frank replaced Trevor Cherry, who would go on to cement positions in central defence and midfield. When you are a striker, though, switching is not so easy in any era. You only have to see how former Leeds star Alan Smith has failed to fit in at both Manchester United and Newcastle.

For many years, Leeds had a tried and tested formula in terms of a forward line with Clarke-Jones before Jordan filled in for the injured Jones. Keegan-Toshack (Liverpool) is the other great double act that always springs to mind and proved a match for any of the partnerships throughout my career as a professional footballer, starting with Osgood-Hutchinson (Chelsea). Ossie was a big man, great in the air and good on the deck. Hutchinson was a workhorse, battering ram and a whirlwind throw-in machine. Other impressive striking line-ups were Chivers-Gilzean (Tottenham), Summerbee-Bell-Lee (Manchester City), Richards-Dougan (Wolves) and Kennedy-Radford (Arsenal).

Clarke picked up his nickname Sniffer because of an ability to poach goals and played off Jones. The duo was the benchmark at Leeds. Jones, and more recently, Jordan was the Trojan while Clarke had a record that could only be admired as a sharpshooter. Fitting into the striking role was problematic for me because Allan and I played a roaming role. I knew opposing managers would cite me as a danger man because of my ability to open up defences, but where most sides preferred marking poacher-type players like Allan, they rarely faced a player like me on a weekly basis. I was a luxury player and knew it. Different strike partnerships offered contrasting problems for defences, and players had to adapt every week. Jimmy utilised me though I was aware he preferred the safe option of Clarke-Jordan and when my strike rate dipped there was only ever going to be one outcome. Bar injury, I'd be used as an impact player.

After our poor start to the campaign, results had picked up. We'd moved up the table but our title defence never got off the ground, although on our day we could match any team in cup clashes. My prospects were brighter when Don Howe arrived from Arsenal as assistant manager. Jimmy, at last, had someone to share the burden and decisions. It also brought a new meaning to the training routine. Don brought a fresh attitude and new ideas to training. His knowledge of the game was outstanding but even his presence failed to get me a starting place in the big games.

During March, we played 11 games including four FA Cup ties against Ipswich Town and two European Cup clashes with Anderlecht. I was in the first team for league games but still suspended when we defeated Anderlecht 3–0 at a foggy Elland Road before Billy scored the solitary goal in horrendous conditions in the return. I was not impressed with Anderlecht and certainly would not have wagered a bet I'd be playing for them within 18 months. Maybe our name was on the FA Cup after I helped us despatch non-league Wimbledon and Derby County courtesy of own goals by Dave Bassett and David Nish, but come the quarter-final at Ipswich Town, I was back on the bench.

Bobby Robson had assembled a terrific side at Ipswich and they were one of the most entertaining teams around to watch and play against with the likes of Trevor Whymark, Clive Woods, Mick Mills, Allan Hunter, Brian Talbot, George Burley and Paul Mariner gaining terrific reputations. All these lads were influential and Ipswich were becoming a top side. Left back Kevin Beattie was the one player who was head and shoulders above everyone else. Possessing pace, strength, touch and natural ability for the game, Beattie would have become an all-time great for England but injuries ultimately wrecked a glittering career.

Prior to the clash at Portman Road, I was exasperated with the boss when I found myself dropped. I was livid and let Jimmy know in no uncertain terms. It did not make sense to me because in a cup game, especially away from home, chances are rare. One moment of magic could prove the difference. My game was built on the unexpected. Facing a big stopper was my scene and it was a huge blow to miss such a high profile game. Leeds scraped a 0–0 draw so Jimmy felt vindicated, but he had a disgruntled player on his hands.

I was on the bench a few days later for the replay at a packed Elland Road. I was again not happy with the decision but had to accept it. The clash would prove a night to remember for me. Leeds fans remember my impact after I came on with 20 minutes to go. Papers dubbed me Super Sub after I struck in the last minute of normal time, racing from halfway before volleying home first time to equalise. Leeds had been out of the Cup when suddenly we went into extra time. We thought that our luck was in when Alan Hunter deflected a shot into his net for an own goal, but the referee chalked it off. We felt robbed by the referee and my last gasp goal was the most memorable I notched for Leeds and lifted the roof at Elland Road.

I hoped for a recall but pulled on the number 12 shirt for the second replay at Filbert Street. Neither side could break the deadlock, though Jordan and Whymark went close. Beattie kicked me up in the air when I joined the action, but we did not get the penalty award that could have taken us through so we had to try for a fourth time. In what proved to be an epic encounter again at Filbert Street we lost 3–2 when Woods scored a late winner. I was gutted both with the result and for not being given a chance to start any of the ties.

By the business end of our season, all talk was of the European Cup semi-final against Barcelona led by legendary playmaker Johan Cruyff. I hoped to get a spot in the team but deep down I knew Jimmy would go for experience. In my opinion a manager should always play the in-form players but the spectre of Revie loomed large so I feared the worst when the team was announced. Again, I was left disappointed when Jimmy put me on the bench. Lorimer was also none too happy to be omitted. But on a fantastic night for the club, Bremner opened the scoring, only for Barcelona to equalise before Clarke scored a late winner in a 2–1 victory.

Between the two ties, I played in 2–1 wins over Arsenal and Ipswich Town but injured my collarbone in the latter triumph at Elland Road when Carl Harris made a scoring debut off the bench for me. I didn't travel to Barcelona and the injury would keep me out of the final two league games. At the Nou Camp, Lorimer started and scored a crucial early goal in a 1–1 draw. Leeds had reached their first European Cup final but they would be without centre half Gordon McQueen who was sent off late on as the pressure mounted. It was a major blow. McQueen was devastated as the lads celebrated a historic triumph.

Whilst conversation at Elland Road centred on the European Cup final, all I concentrated on was getting fit. I played well in friendly matches prior to the final. Against Scotland U23, a makeshift Leeds team claimed the spoils. Paul

Reaney and I were the only first team squad members to play alongside youngsters such as Carl Harris, Glan Letheren and David McNiven as a number of our lads were involved in the Scotland versus England match at Hampden Park. Alfie Conn impressed so much for Scotland U23 that he was selected for the full side 24 hours later. We then played Celtic at Parkhead to keep the show rolling. We won again. I came off at half time, as Jimmy was giving everyone a game. After changing, I met Jock Stein, which was terrific. I was totally in awe of the great man. Jock invited me into his office for a cup of tea. We chatted away as if we were long lost friends.

In the European Cup final at the Parc des Princes in Paris we faced Bayern Munich. I'd recovered from my collarbone injury and realised the best I could hope for was a place on the bench. Jimmy duly selected me for a substitute spot. His reasoning though was bizarre as he based his team selection on the fact that this was Revie's team's last chance to win the European Cup. I told Jimmy he should pick his best team. Sentiment was irrelevant. If Muller or Beckenbauer were not totally fit, Bayern's coach would not be thinking sentimentally. They would not be playing. Jimmy told me I was central to team plans next season at which point I lost it and told him that I was chuffing off. My remark was hot headed and I knew within seconds I'd still be around at the club. I was just frustrated because the biggest honour in Europe was at stake.

The final turned out to be one of the most infamous in the club's history. On the night, Leeds dominated possession, had a cast iron penalty turned down when Beckenbauer fouled Clarke, Lorimer had a goal harshly ruled out and Bremner saw a shot saved at point blank range. Bayern won 2–0 with goals from Roth and Muller while crowd trouble from a section of Leeds supporters destroyed the club's reputation. Nobody could justify the disgraceful scenes created by so-called fans that night, which in turn disgraced the club, but it is safe to say that the referee's dreadful decisions provoked them.

When I look back on that night in Paris, the overriding moment that still rankles is not so much the initial line-up but rather when Jimmy chose not to throw me on in attack when we were desperate for a goal late on. We were losing when Jimmy replaced injured midfielder Terry Yorath with Eddie Gray. In his prime, Eddie was a match winner, but he did not carry the danger that he used to do. I was fresh and could have made an impact against a tired defence. It would have made far more sense to let me loose rather than a winger trying to create an opening. We may still have lost but Jimmy missed an opportunity to have a real go. Jimmy should have taken a risk because I may have changed the course of the match. Jimmy, in my view, bottled it. He sat back and puffed on his pipe as if to say, 'Right, all the Revie lads have had a go.' I was flabbergasted.

That match was the biggest disappointment of my career because I genuinely felt that I'd have made a difference. We needed a goal and Jimmy should have put another striker on. People said afterwards that Jordan was our best player but because of Joe, everything went route one and we did not have another outlay. In the modern game, Alex Ferguson would never hesitate in pulling off his big hitters. If Rooney, Ronaldo, Giggs and the like need resting, so be it. At the time, Leeds had a squad just as strong as Alex Ferguson's. Jimmy should have used his substitutes to better effect. In the dressing room, we were devastated. Putting aside my own feelings of disappointment, I had to feel for the lads who had grown up under Revie. They were all inconsolable. A reception at our Paris hotel was downbeat and the post-match analysis was all about the crowd trouble. Credit to Jimmy, he got a four-year ban halved but that was too late for the Revie lads. The result was truly the end of an era.

Jimmy could now break up the team. Terry Cooper had already joined Middlesbrough, while Giles would soon depart for West Brom as player-manager and Jones' career was all but over through injury. I looked ahead to the 1975–76 season hoping for better fortune, and I went into it feeling confident. After all, I'd been named in the PFA Division 1 side for the first time despite my stop-start efforts during the season. I must have been doing something right.

I was in with the big boys and felt privileged to be in a fantastic XI that read: Peter Shilton (Stoke City), Paul Madeley (Leeds United), Kevin Beattie (Ipswich Town), Billy Bonds (West Ham), Gordon McQueen (Leeds United), Colin Todd (Derby County), Duncan McKenzie (Leeds United), Colin Bell (Manchester City), Bob Latchford (Everton), Alan Hudson (Stoke City) and Leighton James (Burnley).

Peter Shilton was renowned as arguably the best keeper around at the time. Only Pat Jennings and Ray Clemence came close, but Peter got the nod from his peers. Commanding in his penalty area and a great shot stopper, Peter was a fantastic keeper. Paul Madeley could have made the line-up in around half a dozen positions, such was his versatility and I knew all about that, having played alongside him during the season. Kevin Beattie was a player everyone thought could be the next Bobby Moore. Strong as an ox, a hard tackler as well as fast, a glittering career was in front of him until injuries wrecked his career. Billy Bonds was underrated as an England prospect. I knew how that felt, but he was respected by players in the game while everyone knew the potential of Gordon McQueen as a reliable stopper and dangerous header of the ball at set pieces.

Colin Todd was a proven top class defender and Derby's key

player during their title-winning season. When Cloughie paid £170,000 for Colin, pundits went berserk but the great man knew what he was doing. In midfield, Colin Bell was still in his prime. Nicknamed Nijinsky because of his work rate and ability to run all day, Colin had much more to his game and was another class act. Blessed with a lovely first touch, he spotted openings and scored on a regular basis. I was delighted to see another so-called maverick, Alan Hudson, make the side because he was a fantastic player in the middle of the park, while left winger Leighton James, apart from scoring goals aplenty, would have supplied the ammunition for a future Everton strike partnership of Latchford-McKenzie. Bob was such a strong lad and a terrific leader of the line. The current England team would have their work cut out to beat this line-up, even with Rooney and Walcott on song.

Pre-season, I felt very much a part of things at Elland Road. The lads had nicknamed me 'Precious' McKenzie after a British weightlifter at the time and it was not long before my party trick of jumping over a Mini came to the fore. I was partly to blame for this because I just happened to mention my bizarre caper to some of the lads in passing and, of course, it was not long before I was ribbed. The lads were somewhat disbelieving and I can't blame them. They wanted to see if I could match up to my claims and I was happy to oblige. One of the receptionists owned a Mini so a date was set and club secretary Keith Archer recorded the audacious vault. I jumped over the Mini amid gasps of disbelief, but the manager was not impressed. Jimmy immediately banned my party trick in case I was injured larking about and I understood his reasoning. On the other hand, I was pleased as I'd settled a few side wagers.

On the field I was raring to go and appreciated the talent I was playing alongside. Skipper Billy Bremner was past his peak but was still first pick on the team sheet and what a leader he was for club and country. I've never experienced anyone quite like Billy before or since on a football pitch. When Billy pulled on the white shirt of Leeds United, you could sense the pride he felt, even though he'd played hundreds of games. He led from the front and I'd seen him give teammates a rollicking for a misplaced pass but he was also the first to pat them on the back. Billy also had the habit of popping up for crucial goals and was always in the thick of the action. Billy's partnership with Johnny Giles was telepathic but I only witnessed it first hand on a few occasions as Giles had moved on to pastures new during the close season. Giles had two great feet, an amazing football brain and was a wonderful passer of the ball. Johnny could find a player from any distance with consummate accuracy and ease.

In goal, David Harvey was a real character as he had a smallholding in North Yorkshire where he bred greyhounds and rabbits. We always knew when Suave was around because he had a pair of wellies in his car and we could smell the countryside. A Scotland regular, David was a solid keeper. I never saw him flying around unnecessarily and he did not look spectacular between the sticks but David was very efficient.

Paul Reaney was always bubbly in the dressing room. He was a real character and nicknamed Stan after Stanley Matthews as he played down the right. Stan was forever cracking jokes with the lads from the minute he arrived at the ground. On the park, Paul had raw pace and was a solid right back. Very few wingers got the better of him. He was also continuously looking for a deal to benefit the lads and has not changed much since then. Paul currently works as an agent for the lads organising speaking engagements and coaching sessions. The banter is always terrific both on the park and on the after-dinner circuit. Left back Frank Gray was very skilful. Frank had a big act to follow not only in terms of his brother Eddie but also following Terry Cooper because Terry was arguably the best there had been in recent years.

Leeds were spoilt for choice in the centre of defence. When it came to reputations, Norman 'Bites Yer Legs' Hunter had arguably the fiercest reputation in the game. His tackling was legendary on the park but he was a pussycat off it. On the field Norman was a born winner and very aggressively determined. He was from the same school as Ron Harris and Tommy Smith. All three lived up to the reputation and I still have the scars to prove it! Harris and Smith were genuine hard men but neither had determination like Norman possessed. Although he lacked natural pace, Norman never got credit for the skill he had. I played with and against Norman and he had tremendous ability. A great player, Norman would have won far more England caps but for vying for the same shirt as Bobby Moore. His consistency was justifiably rewarded when he won the Players Player of the Year award in 1973.

Gordon McQueen lined up alongside Norman. A budding Scottish international, Gordon had been a regular for a couple of seasons but was already regarded as one of the best young centre backs around. Blessed with great timing for a big man, he was also quick to retaliate, which got him into trouble on occasions. Powerful in the air, Gordon was a danger whether defending or joining the attack at set pieces. We affectionately called him 'Beastie' and he was some sprinter when in full flight. Gordon was arguably the quickest footballer playing league football at that time. Once in his stride, he was an absolute flying machine.

Paul Madeley was another first pick on the team sheet. Throughout my spell at Leeds, Paul was my roommate and we were complete opposites. Whereas I was a jack-in-the-box character, Paul was totally laid-back but on the field he was a superb player. Dubbed Mr Versatile due to his uncanny knack of being able to slot into numerous positions, Paul predominantly played full back, centre half or in front of the back four in midfield, but incredibly, he played in every outfield position during his career. I faced Paul in his man-marker role and he was almost impossible to shake off. With pace to burn, most of the time Paul ran around in only second or third gear. He never seemed to have to go into overdrive. Paul was also known as the Rolls Royce of footballers and I would not argue with that accolade. Paul is, for me, the best utility player the game has produced.

Key members of the squad were also Eddie Gray, Trevor Cherry and Terry Yorath. But for injuries, Eddie would have been one of the greats of all time and he would have won many more Scottish caps than he achieved. Eddie had incredible ball control, balance and timing. When fit, there was no finer sight that Eddie running at a full back and his dribbling skills set up many goals. An old clip of his goal against Burnley in 1970 when he beat defender after defender in the penalty box before slotting the ball home is a classic and shows him at his magical best. Eddie was undoubtedly the next best thing to George Best.

Trevor filled in as a right-footed left back and also excelled elsewhere along the back line in addition to midfield where he was renowned for breaking up attacks. As for Terry, he had just cemented a place in the side after being on the fringes as an understudy to Bremner or Giles for many years. Terry was a fine player but replacing the likes of Giles was an impossible task. Fans did not appreciate his efforts, but the lads did, and sadly he became a target for the boo boys as the club rebuilt. Terry went on to serve other clubs and remained a first choice for Wales, captaining the side many times.

King of the strikers was Allan Clarke who, after Jimmy

Greaves, was arguably the best English finisher the game had seen at that particular time. Dubbed Sniffer for his clinical finishing ability, Allan passed the ball into the net rather than blasting it. His assassin reputation was fully justified because when Allan was one on one with a keeper, you knew he'd score. Peter Lorimer had a thunderbolt of a shot. Sometimes myths are exaggerated when pundits talk about players, but the power of Hotshot Lorimer's shot was amazing. In fact, he was not allowed to shoot against Leeds' keepers in training because of the risk of injury to them. It was not just his shooting ability that made Peter a danger, his range of passes was superb. Peter was not the quickest or trickiest on the right wing but he invariably supplied the final ball despite appearing to be in the wrong situation. As a player he was deservedly renowned for his shooting ability for club and country.

Joe Jordan was gaining a reputation as a fearsome leader of the line when I arrived at Elland Road, but Joe became a better player when he left Leeds for Manchester United in 1978. When I partnered Joe, he seemed more intent on getting into a scrap with centre-halves as opposed to knocking the ball in the back of the net. As a result he did not score the goals he ought to have done. Immensely strong in the air and in possession, Joe gave opposing centre-halves a torrid time. Big Joe succeeded Mick Jones and was among the great strong running centre forwards of his generation alongside the likes of Malcolm Macdonald and Bob Latchford. At Old Trafford, Joe blossomed and went on to become a world class centre-forward. He later starred in Italy, which was no mean feat, and was a talisman for Scotland at three World Cups.

Joe was thick as thieves with his big mate Gordon McQueen. Both were among the few players from the Revie era to excel after they left the club, much to the annoyance of Leeds supporters. But in the late seventies, Leeds were not the force they once were and both these Scots were coming to their prime so you could not blame them for looking for new challenges. Joe and Gordon were great finds from Scottish minnows Morton and St Mirren. Lining up against this duo was a frightening prospect for opponents, especially for a defender facing Big Joe running at full flight. Also, at corner kicks and free kicks they were both a handful. Their presence left room for players such as me to strike. The big boys looked for McQueen and Jordan, not a butterfly like McKenzie to sneak in unnoticed.

Come the opening game of the 1975–76 season, I was in at the start as Jordan was sidelined for potentially a long lay off. Injuries are part and parcel of the game and players never wish them on teammates, but I was determined to make an impact. Lorimer got our campaign off to a flyer with a brace in a 2–1 win at Aston Villa before a Lash special saw off Ipswich Town. Liverpool, with Bob Paisley replacing Bill Shankly at the helm and building an Anfield dynasty, taught us a footballing lesson at Elland Road when they won 3–0. Determined to bounce back, I got on the score sheet in successive victories over Sheffield United and Wolves before another strike helped account for Ipswich in the League Cup. Clarke was also on target against Town with the winner and another predatory strike by Sniffer set us on the way to a 2–1 win over Queens Park Rangers to make it six wins in 10 games as clubs noted we meant business.

One problem we did have was the imminent absence of McQueen after he picked up a bad knock against Rangers. With Madeley in the squad we had a readymade replacement but there was also added pressure on Yorath without the flair of Giles. Terry battled away in midfield and had to ignore barracking from some home fans. I was delighted when Terry sealed a 3–0 win over Newcastle after I'd notched a couple of strikes. My goal scoring touch continued with two in another three-goal win over Birmingham City.

Jimmy Armfield had believed in me the previous season when we defeated Arsenal at Elland Road just after he took the helm. And the Gunners found themselves on the end of another McKenzie double but this time at Highbury as we claimed a noteworthy 2–1 triumph. The result was particularly pleasant. I was pleased with my performance, but a number of Arsenal's promising youngsters impressed me, in particular midfielder Liam Brady who would star for the Republic of Ireland in years to come.

Brady was just a kid in the Arsenal line-up that day. I remember nutmegging him and giving him a little wink as I went off on a run. Ten minutes later, the cheeky little bugger returned the compliment by nutmegging me before turning around and giving me a wink. I thought, 'Good on yer son, you're gonna be some player.' Reputations meant nothing to Liam and he duly became a classy midfielder blessed with fantastic technique, a terrific engine and a great left peg. He starred in the 1979 FA Cup final when Arsenal defeated Manchester United in a thriller at Wembley and went on to become one of the best English-based exports to Italian football. Liam was what pundits would describe as one of those players who could open a can of peas with his left foot.

Despite a setback at Ipswich, three successive wins took us into the festive fixtures in a great frame of mind. Matches always come thick and fast during this period and supporters dressed up suitably as our good form continued. Sniffer settled a tight game at home to Aston Villa with a typical strike to send fans home in fine voice on our march up the table before Christmas. While Leeds supporters tucked into Christmas pudding, we prepared for a tough encounter at Manchester City. And

Madeley came up trumps to secure a Boxing Day victory. Twenty-four hours later in front of our biggest attendance of the season at Elland Road, I struck twice in a 4–0 win as we thumped Leicester City to end a torrid year on a high.

The New Year always starts with the FA Cup and we were determined not to come unstuck at Notts County in the third round. Another Sniffer strike made sure of that before Billy and I struck to see off Stoke City in the league and make it five victories on the bounce. Everything seemed set for a terrific second half of the season but injuries to Bremner and Lorimer hit the balance of the side. Billy was sidelined in a shock FA Cup defeat to Crystal Palace when flamboyant manager Malcolm Allison grabbed the headlines and Billy's continued absence in the middle of the park coincided with three back-to-back defeats. The last, by Middlesbrough at home, saw Lorimer pick up an injury that would all but finish his season.

Injuries are part and parcel of football yet, when they hit key individuals, they can have a debilitating effect as a team looks for consistency. Jordan came back into the fray but one victory at Coventry City during a run of 10 league games wrecked any chance of a title challenge that looked possible at Christmas. Billy's return to the side after two months just before Easter brought a resurgence in form. Although he was not fully fit, his influence had an effect on all the lads. Suddenly the swagger was back in the side and results began to come our way again as we racked up straight victories to overcome Everton, Arsenal, Newcastle and Burnley. Billy set the standards with goals at Goodison and against the Gunners, while I was happy to get back on the score sheet in a 2–1 victory over Burnley.

Our season, however, was petering out and one victory over Manchester City during the last five games saw us finish fifth, which was not a bad achievement after the traumatic previous season. Although it had not been the most glorious campaign in the club's history, supporters had been entertained at different stages of the season and I was delighted how my season had gone, especially as I finished top scorer with 17 goals. Jimmy Armfield was slowly guiding the club through a very difficult period.

Away from action on the park, if I thought my Mini jumping days were over, I was wrong. Paul Reaney persuaded me to be the main attraction before his testimonial match. Around 12,000 fans were on hand to witness my jump and, come the day of the jump, I had plenty of nerves as I'd only done it before in front of five or six people, not in front of thousands. The owner of the Mini would not get out of his car for insurance purposes so had a crash helmet on. Running up to jump over the Mini, I thought to myself, 'Why have I agreed to do this?' and brushed the car on the way down. That was my last Mini jump but it was caught on camera for posterity and I enjoy signing copies of the photo as a memento of the day for fans. Jimmy Armfield came over to me. 'Very impressive Duncan, we've paid £250,000 for your services, don't do it again.' I must thank Jim one day!

With Mini jumping officially over, one party trick remained. This was my ability to throw a golf ball a long way. Again the lads ribbed me about it, so when Norman Hunter challenged me to throw a golf ball over the top of the West Stand at Elland Road, my competitive instincts re-emerged. I'm not normally a betting man but I knew that I couldn't lose and there was no way I could refuse to take on Norman's bet. Norman was not happy when he saw the ball fly over the stand way into the distance. The look on his face was a picture.

Towards the end of the season, rumours were rife that Leeds were considering letting me go. They were desperate for a midfield playmaker and keen to sign Tony Currie from Sheffield

United. My departure would finance the deal. Anderlecht approached Leeds about my availability. They had played Wrexham during a run to the European Cup Winners Cup final when they beat West Ham 4–2 and said the Wrexham tie was the hardest clash. The Dutch giants had enquired about Billy Ashcroft but it didn't work out.

Jimmy informed me Anderlecht were interested in signing me and that the club had agreed a £200,000 fee. Jimmy wanted to know my thoughts. I was top scorer at Leeds, but still felt the odd man out of four strikers. Playing abroad appealed to me. Not many British players had been successful in another country, so it was a challenge. Financially I knew that I'd be better off. Discussing it with Dot, it was not a difficult decision, just as it had not been a difficult decision to leave Nottingham Forest. I could have stayed and battled for my place but I was not in Jimmy's long term plans and knew that it was time to move on.

Before I knew it, I was at a Leeds hotel with a six-strong delegation from Anderlecht including an interpreter. Negotiations went smoothly especially as I spoke French, thanks to my school days when I got an A in my 'O' level, but I did not let them know that (I became fluent in French whilst living in Belgium). I signed on a similar wage to the wage I was on at Leeds but the bonuses were phenomenal. Moving arrangements were also included. After we'd agreed terms, club officials said I'd stretched them and that they didn't think we'd agree at one stage, but I knew the maximum the club were prepared to pay so asked for that. Anderlecht announced the deal at a press conference with club president Constant van den Stock and manager Raymond Goethals.

As I contemplated pastures new, I was privileged to make the PFA Division 1 side for the second year in a row and gain recognition from my playing peers for a third successive year, giving me a memorable hat-trick. As in 1975, it was some line-up with a number of other great players making the side again. The full line-up was: Pat Jennings (Tottenham Hotspur), Paul Madeley (Leeds United), Kevin Beattie (Ipswich Town), Don Masson (Queens Park Rangers), Roy McFarland (Derby County), Colin Todd (Derby County), Kevin Keegan (Liverpool), Alan Hudson (Stoke City), Duncan McKenzie (Leeds United), John Toshack (Liverpool) and Dennis Tueart (Manchester City).

I played against fantastic keepers during my career, including Gordon Banks and Peter Shilton, but a school of thought by many players was that Pat Jennings was just ahead of both these goalkeeping giants. Big Pat was a tremendous keeper and repeatedly pulled off terrific saves. For me there was little to choose between the trio. They all had different styles, commanded the penalty area with authority and were terrific shot-stoppers but when Big Pat caught the ball for the umpteenth time one-handed, pundits, players and supporters realised it was no fluke. Big Pat was strong, had hands like shovels and for me was marginally better than both Banksy and Shilts, although I would not have wanted to be the manager to choose between them.

I'd been selected alongside Madeley, Beattie, Todd and Hudson 12 months earlier, while Masson and Tueart had been in the Division 2 XI in 1974. Although it was only a dream team, for me it was terrific to find myself recognised once again. And what a line-up the players voted for on this occasion. A stalwart with Derby and England, Roy McFarland was in the side partnering Todd in defence. They were a fantastic combination and terrific international footballers.

Liverpool duo Kevin Keegan and John Toshack completed the line-up as twin strikers. Keegan worked defenders to submission, but for me he was far better than just a hard working player as many pundits judged him. I thought this judgement was unfair at times. Kevin certainly worked hard at his game and developed a great touch on the ball but he was also a terrific finisher. Undeniably, though, Kevin was never better than when he combined with Toshack. Toshack had incredible belief in his ability, was a powerful runner, was aerially superb and proved to be a handful for any defender. Both were winners through and through and this showed on the field. They made their name in the Bill Shankly team and continued under Bob Paisley.

Looking back at my spell at Leeds United it's too easy to say that Don Revie was an impossible act to follow. Change had to occur, and credit goes to Jimmy Armfield because he did steady the ship. However, for me Jimmy was more the perfect neighbour than the hard-hitting manager, and it did not surprise me when he found his feet as a respected journalist and broadcaster after departing Leeds. Jimmy was, and has remained, a consummate diplomat who finds a way to say the right thing at a crucial juncture. Jimmy was a brilliant mediator at Elland Road, but I have never been convinced he really enjoyed the post. I think his ideal managerial job would have been at his former club, Blackpool, which he graced for years.

Despite the pressures and club politics associated with managing a club the size of Leeds, Jimmy made his mark and retained a sharp sense of humour. One match day, he quipped with a wry smile, 'Duncan, try and change your normal game today . . . play well!' And on another occasion, Jimmy, looking at my boots, commented ' . . . do they run on their own? I hope so because you chuffing don't help them.' Jimmy always had a sharp line. I enjoyed his company and still do when I see him on my travels. For me, though, during the summer of 1976, I realised that you are soon yesterday's hero and my next challenge was across the Channel.

6

BELGIUM BLISS

Moving abroad to play football was a rarity in 1976 for British footballers. Prior to my departure, only a few British players had tried their luck abroad, the most high profile players being John Charles (Juventus), Jimmy Greaves (AC Milan) and Denis Law (AC Milan). It had been well over a decade since anyone had played overseas so it was big news in England at the time. I was also the first British player to play in Belgium. The standard was, by all accounts, much like Scotland with a couple of big clubs dominating. Anderlecht and FC Bruges were the equivalent to Celtic and Rangers competing for top spot.

It would be a challenge because I was used to physical encounters each week but now, apart from playing against the equal of a top lower league side on a regular basis, I'd have to get used to facing opponents with 10 men behind the ball. And it would prove tough to break down. Teams defended deep when they visited Anderlecht so by all accounts at home it was not unusual to win a close encounter and be booed by your own fans.

R.S.C. Anderlecht had a number of world class stars including Dutch duo Arie Haan and Robbie Rensenbrink who starred in the 1974 World Cup with Johan Cruyff and Johan Neeskens. In goal was Jan Ruiter, Francois Van Der Elst was a key player in defence alongside Jean Dockx while midfielder

Ludo Coeck would have become the best Belgium player of all time had he not tragically died in a motor accident before he reached his prime. Haan was the most medalled player at the time in football and was a class act when combined with Rensenbrink. I lined up as the lone striker or off a front man.

Pre-season training was nothing like in England. I was used to physical training, but all the squad did was a short cross-country run and a few planned moves. Fitness-wise there was no problem, but it was a different game on the field to anything I had been used to back home. Playing in Belgium would prove an education. Every aspect of training was so different to the English game. I learned more in five days at Anderlecht than five years in England. We took our match kit, training kit and boots home every day. We had our own football, training boots, match boots and various kits. Everything was a player's responsibility and to me it made sense. Apart from the game being more technical, I knew that the intensity of a match was the complete opposite to a helter-skelter game in England. Playing with naturally gifted players in terms of touch on the ball would give me an appreciation of continental football and hopefully improve my game.

Anderlecht appointed Raymond Goethals as manager just before my arrival. Previously he had been in charge of the national team for a decade. Goethals was a controversial figure and spoke his mind (very much in the Cloughie mould) which did not go down well with supporters. The media boys loved his press conferences. Goethals was a disciplinarian and that suited me. From training to diet and match day preparation, everything was planned and organised. Goethals also banned smoking on the team coach but that did not apply to him as he puffed away at the front. Being the type of character I was, it did not take me long to test his ruling immediately with a sneaky cigarette. I was instantly disciplined, and then appealed but that did not faze Goethals as his ban was on all players!

One aspect of the manager that surprised me was that he did not change the dress code on match days. I was used to wearing a suit but the order of the day at Anderlecht was jeans and a t-shirt. I got plenty of ribbing in the early days so was happy to follow the club attire. Goethals was not a fan of foreign imports but realised he had star players, especially with Rensenbrink who was the best striker in Belgian football. As Goethals was involved in my arrival, I was given a chance to impress. He was passionate about football, lived and breathed the sport but was not interested in off the field luxuries that football offered. Goethals lived in a modest apartment, drove an old car and wore the same suit daily.

Anderlecht had a great team, arguably the best Belgium club side there has been. At the time, they were also one of the best in Europe. My debut came in the Super Cup final. The game brought together Bayern Munich, who claimed the European Cup for a third successive time, on this occasion defeating St Etienne, and European Cup Winners Cup winners Anderlecht who had overcome West Ham. Although not one of the 'big three' European trophies (the UEFA Cup being the third) the Super Cup was a high profile game. We lost 2–1 in Munich and bizarrely before the return, there was a small matter of agreeing incentives to win the coveted trophy. George Denil negotiated between the players and Anderlecht board. A multi-millionaire, George imported coffee from South America and looked after the players. Apart from keeping us stocked with the best coffee beans, he enjoyed taking us out for fine meals and always picked up the bill. Rensenbrink and Haan negotiated £5,000 per player if we won, which was serious money in those days.

With an incentive in place, it was game on and we duly

avenged our defeat with a 4–2 win at home to claim the trophy on aggregate. Rensenbrink provided the business on the park with a match winning display. All the big guns such as Beckenbauer, Schwarzenbeck, Muller and Maier played for Bayern but we steamrollered them. Winning gave me the distinction of being the first Englishman to win a Super Cup winners medal. Triumphing was special in spite of it being no more than a high profile pre-season game. Unfortunately, during my career this honour would be my only winners' medal.

The pre-season schedule included free flowing games, in stark comparison to what was around the corner in Belgium football, when we defeated Ajax, Leeds United and Nice. All managers have different styles and Goethals was outspoken even in a friendly. Raimondo, as the press dubbed him, was always good for a quote and during a game let the referee know continually what he felt about decisions. Goethals was non-stop. Against Leeds, he accidentally trod on a trainer's hand when jumping up to argue about a decision, and would soon be in hot water again during a European Cup Winners Cup match against Galatasaray when we were thumping them.

I made my league debut at home in a 1–1 draw against Liuk, which was a disappointing result. It would have been worse if Rensenbrink had not rescued a point. The pace caught me out a little but the overall standard was poor, which matched the bulk of stadiums, although that did not apply to Anderlecht's ground. It was all very different from Old Trafford, Anfield, Highbury and Goodison Park. But it was a challenge and I knew that at least I'd be playing European football, as opposed to my former club who were starting a two-year ban.

Playing a 4–4–2 system with two wingers and me as target man, we relied on a forward breaking from midfield to support the attack. It was a different formation to back home and took me a while to adapt as I felt isolated, but I got on with playing off scraps. League matches initially were a struggle and I only managed to score one goal in the opening eight games. Man-marked, it took me time to get used to the system. Opponents kicked me at every opportunity, but after my experience in the European Cup against Ujpest Dosza with Leeds, I realised that I'd have to bide my time for an opening and not retaliate. A few games without a goal got the press going about my contribution to the team, but all credit to Goethals, he backed both me and the side after a tetchy affair against St Etienne. Results got better as Anderlecht had class players to break opponents down and my form improved.

In the mid seventies, there was little or no opportunity to watch European teams on television. That, of course, has changed beyond all recognition. In fact, modern television coverage was just a pipe dream in 1976. Today, if a player wants to try his luck abroad it's no major deal. There is a mass of material available for a footballer to peruse before committing to a club. Also top players play regularly against European opposition in either the Champions League or UEFA Cup, a competition now called UEFA Europa League as of the 2009-10 season. When clubs opted to play in an end of season competition called the Anglo-Italian Cup in my era, there was much laughter from the likes of Manchester City, Newcastle United, West Ham and Aston Villa. Now teams outside the big four (Manchester United, Chelsea, Liverpool and Arsenal) actively eulogise about the tournament as a gateway into Europe if they finish mid-table but complain when they reach the latter stages due to fixture congestion. That said, players today have it far easier to plan facing European opposition.

Our fiercest opponents were Club Bruges and RWD Molenbeek. Head to head results against both went some way to deciding the destination of the title. Like any big match, the build up for these crucial games was more intense but we also had to be on our guard when playing the likes of Winterslag and Charleroi but not because of danger on the park. Both had supporters with a notorious reputation and I soon experienced it first hand when a controversial last gasp Rensenbrink penalty brought us a deserved win at Winterslag, a little mining village team in the Arden. It had been backs to the wall for Winterslag as we battered them. We warranted a victory but home supporters were having none of it and tried to get into our dressing room to get at both the referee and Anderlecht players. There were a few scary moments when what appeared to be half the local police force turned up to disperse an angry mob.

In reality, Anderlecht were the Manchester United of the Belgium First Division. Every game was a cup final for opponents but one game guaranteed to generate a great atmosphere was the derby clash against Racing White. Although the match did not have quite the passion of an Everton-Liverpool game, as I'd soon discover, Anderlecht-Racing White had an edge, which suited me. Playing away we held a 1–0 lead when the referee gave Racing a number of free kicks late on. Racing equalised in the dying seconds. Goethals was incensed with the referee and let him know at the time and afterwards in post-match interviews. Papers had another headline. There was a standing joke that Raimondo was in the press more than his players.

I'd quickly discovered a major difference in my adopted country. This was that football, by some distance, was not the national sport. In Belgium, cycling took the honour with five-time Tour de France winner Eddie Merckx a clear national sporting hero, although footballer Paul Van Himst was up there in terms of Belgium heroes. Nevertheless, the McKenzie family was welcomed by Anderlecht and the locals were terrific. In fact it got embarrassing at times because Dot and I were guests wherever we went. Anderlecht as a club provided everything. We lived in a luxurious five-bedroom home and I had a courtesy Porsche. I could not ask for a better lifestyle or standard of living. Life was wonderful.

I was part of the foreign legion and lived next door to Arie Haan in a breathtaking part of town. Needless to say I had no complaints, but there was a split in the camp. Being the only English player at Anderlecht, I found myself in a unique position. The Belgium lads saw me as little threat compared to the Dutch players, but they did have a sense of feeling hard done by because the foreign brigade had better salaries and a more salubrious lifestyle. The result was that the Belgium lads stuck together as did the Dutch players. I managed to get on with both groups. They always liked a laugh and a joke and my range of comedy was Irish gags. Luckily I had plenty in the locker. All the lads enjoyed my repertoire so I needed a constant supply of gags to keep 'em laughing.

For a professional footballer, off-the-field activities were beginning to change, especially in Europe. Back home, a number of lads had interests in a pub or fashion outlet but the level of entrepreneurial activity was generally limited. Many players relied on a testimonial to provide for a rainy day, but that was not the attitude on the continent. It was not uncommon for footballers to have outside business interests in a variety of areas and the Dutch lads, especially, embraced the revolution. They owned properties and loved fast cars but come match day, players had to set aside financial aspirations.

My popularity among both players and the Anderlecht faithful was thankfully developing, which made me even more determined to entertain supporters when given the opportunity by improvising with tricks and flicks. As at previous clubs, teammates could not always read my game so I was viewed as more an individual than a team player. I'd heard it all before but was determined to persevere. Our star player was Rensenbrink and to be fair, Robbie scored a stack of goals to justify his status. He was tremendously skilful. Possessing a sublime left foot and a great ability in the air, Rensenbrink could play for fun.

Back in England, my career was being tracked as it was such a novelty having an English player plying his trade abroad. British journalists flew over to interview me with questions regarding all aspects of my lifestyle. Among them were Ian Carnaby from Radio 5 (these were the days before 5 Live) and the late Brian Moore of ITV. My lifestyle was clearly better than players' lifestyle in England. Our home was stunning, but the kitchen was tiny because the norm was to go out and eat. Belgian cuisine was renowned as being among the best. Locals did not shout about it like the French but the food was delightful.

I'd adjusted to life in Europe yet few players in Britain seemed tempted to try their luck abroad. One of the biggest obstacles was the language barrier. My basic French became fluent inside three months, which to me was essential. Times and opinions were beginning to change in England and the coming years would see Kevin Keegan, Trevor Francis, Tony Woodcock, Joe Jordan and Graeme Souness make an impact. Keegan was the most successful player. A leading light for Liverpool as well as England captain, Kevin would star at SV Hamburg following a £500,000 transfer, winning the European Player of the Year award. But Kevin took time to settle as there was some resentment from teammates. Kevin was, and still is, a tremendous ambassador for the game.

On the field, I was contributing more and more. I soon found myself on the way to scoring 16 goals in 30 games, which would go some way to scooping the supporters' Player of the Year award. I was pleased with my efforts, loved the lifestyle, was confident in my ability to entertain and of hitting my goal target, when news came from home that my father-in-law had been diagnosed with cancer. Dot naturally wanted to return home to Derby. I stayed on in Brussels while the football season continued, but my idealist lifestyle was suddenly not quite so ideal. The club understood my predicament and offered support, which I appreciated.

During an international weekend get-together, the Dutch squad had a training camp near Amsterdam. I was planning to have a quiet few days in our apartment when Ronnie Rensenbrink and Arie Haan approached me with other plans. They invited me to join the Dutch training camp. I was amazed to hear this but they were genuine. The duo had explained my circumstances to Holland coach Rinus Michels and he readily agreed for me to attend. It didn't take them long to persuade me. I packed my kit and drove with them to the camp which would prove a real footballing eye-opener. Rinus recognised me. 'Ah McKenzie, you have shoes, [he meant boots], good, come and train with us.'

I didn't face Johan Cryuff in a competitive match but this was the next best thing. Training with the Dutch Nations Cup squad was an amazing experience. Seeing first hand just how talented the Dutch players were was wonderful. Technically they were superb. It has always puzzled me how Holland failed to win the World Cup in 1974 and 1978. During this period they were, for me, the best team in the world but lost out to West Germany and then Argentina. During both tournaments, Holland were the most technically gifted team and the 1974 Dutch squad was the greatest of my era. The class of 1974 had everything . . . touch, pace, style and a cutting edge. Everyone talks about the great Brazilian team of 1970 that played exhilarating football. These lads also played 'total' football with Cruyff being the star player.

Ball players were encouraged in Holland. All top sides had a fantastic youth policy, especially Ajax who dominated European football in the early seventies along with Feyenoord. Flair players like Worthington, Bowles and me would have enjoyed a far greater chance of domestic, maybe even international, recognition if we had grown up in the Dutch system.

When Dot's dad passed away, she naturally wanted to be at home with her mother to offer support. Staying long term at Anderlecht was no longer an option. Club officials understood my predicament but obviously wanted to recoup their investment. West Ham, Rangers and Everton were the main clubs to make enquiries. A move to Everton, in particular, appealed to me for all sorts of reasons although playing for West Ham was attractive because of the style of football they played. Living in London, however, was not an option. All things considered, there was a natural pull towards Goodison Park.

Everton were a club with a rich history but they had not won major honours since 1970 when they were League Champions. Funds were made available to build a team to challenge for Europe. Everton manager Billy Bingham came over with an entourage of officials and local reporters that included Chris James, John Keith, Clive Tyldesley and Elton Welsby to cover my transfer. My move was big news on Merseyside.

Following negotiations, I joined Everton in a £200,000 deal. Everton club secretary Jim Greenwood was amazed when Anderlecht directors came to see me off, but I was not surprised as we got on well. Chairman Costa van den Stock told me that he hoped I'd return one day and I've been back as a guest on a number of occasions. I left with fond memories and shortly after my departure, Anderlecht's manager Goethals moved on to a new post. I remember Raimondo as a great character. It was a fantastic experience living abroad and I'd recommend it to any footballer if they are given the chance but it was time to return to England and top flight football.

Joining Everton was my first choice even though I was worse off financially. I signed for £200 a week but Billy agreed a loyalty bonus that doubled my salary so as not to upset other players on a similar wage. Billy was aware other clubs were sniffing around and wanted to tie up the deal. This meant I had a bargaining chip. Sentiment aside that I wanted to join Everton, it had to be the right deal for my family. My package put me at the higher end of player salaries in English football. A player's career is a short one so I was delighted with the deal. I'd come a long way since my days as an apprentice at Nottingham Forest. Spells at Leeds and Anderlecht had made me a better player. I had more experience and believed that I could make an impact at Goodison Park. I looked forward with anticipation to playing for Everton.

7

MERSEY BEAT BUT WEMBLEY HEARTACHE

When I arrived at Everton in December 1977, I finally found my spiritual home as a footballer. Dot is a true Scouser while my daughter Riah was born in Billinge, a village just a few miles outside Liverpool. Everton fans had endured a miserable ride following an era when they won the FA Cup in 1966 and league title four years later with Brian Labone leading the side. Harry Catterick was manager and supporters idolised the legendary midfield line-up of Ball-Harvey-Kendall and striker Joe Royle. Everton had not come close to the same level of success, enjoying just one top four finish since being crowned champions, but the will was present again to move the club towards those halcyon days.

After signing on the dotted line for Everton, I attended a press conference alongside Bruce Rioch who had joined from Derby County. Bruce was a cultured midfielder and major force when Derby won the Division 1 title in 1975 under my old boss Dave Mackay. Another fine midfielder, Andy King, and I had been signed to beef up the squad. But as a team we had some way to go before matching Liverpool, who had dominated English football for some seasons, winning Division 1, FA Cup and UEFA Cup honours. Attendances were on the slide at Goodison Park so our aim was simple—we had to bring back the feel-good factor to Goodison with results.

Billy joked that when I last joined an English club, Leeds United, the manager was sacked inside a few weeks. He got a laugh but history would soon repeat itself! Of course, none of us knew it at the time as Billy explained how his new signings would get Everton back on track. The three of us travelled to Everton's training ground, Bellefield, to meet our new teammates. Being a central part of a new era at the club was tremendous with Christmas just around the corner. We were determined to restore pride and bring back the glory days to Everton. The first thing was to get myself match fit for Division 1 because at Anderlecht the schedule had been more conditioning work by comparison.

Steve Burtenshaw was among the coaching staff and fast-tracked my training schedule, but I knew sharpness would only return properly with regular first team football. As a footballer, I'd matured following spells at Leeds and Anderlecht. Entertaining supporters with neat flicks and tricks was fine and dandy but my skills needed to be integrated into a winning team. Billy had been granted a war chest to develop the side but unbeknown to the players, behind the scenes, plans were afoot to sack him regardless of results.

I made my debut at Coventry City's Highfield Road ground. We lost 4–2 but the manager was pleased with my contribution and in our next clash at home to Birmingham City, I struck both our goals in a 2–2 draw. Although disappointed we had not won, it was a terrific opening in front of the Everton faithful. During the game, I could sense a tense atmosphere developing due to a poor run of form but all we could do as players was work hard and hope breaks started to come our way.

I was delighted that Evertonians seemed to accept me instantly as one of the new players at the club but being a striker is a double-edged sword. Forwards can be involved in all the build up play imaginable and make terrific runs but they are ultimately judged on scoring goals, rightly so in my opinion. Everton had signed me to score goals and it was my job to deliver them. Only then would supporters look at what else I offered the side. I'd proved a reliable goal-getter at my previous clubs and had matured as a player so was more determined than ever to succeed.

My strike partner in attack was Big Bob Latchford, a £350,000 signing from Birmingham City in 1974. In the seventies, Bob was one of the best leaders of the line and that suited my style. At Leeds United, I was at my best playing off Joe Jordan, at Anderlecht I was the lone striker, now I had a chance again to pick up the pieces from Bob's barnstorming runs leading the line and prowess in the air. My inventiveness could also set up Bob with chances, as he was a natural goal scorer. A Latchford-McKenzie combination was potentially lethal.

While our fledgling partnership developed, our overall form was poor and over the festive period we suffered a Boxing Day 4–0 drubbing at Manchester United. Although Old Trafford was not the magnificent stadium it is today, running out in front of 56,000 plus fans was an experience to relish. Playing before packed houses is what the game is all about. Despite this we got a thumping that day. Determined to bounce back, a 2–2 draw with Middlesbrough was not quite the result we wanted but the New Year was around the corner and that meant the FA Cup.

For all footballers back then, the FA Cup was a terrific competition because it gave teams a chance to play in the biggest game of the season at Wembley. In the modern era, playing at Wembley is still a thrill but so many games take place at the hallowed stadium now, even FA Cup semi-finals, that some of the magic has been taken away. Back in the seventies, outside of England international games, only the FA Cup, League Cup and Charity Shield were staged at Wembley so there was the Holy Grail element for footballers. To play at the Twin Towers was a massive goal and I'd already experienced it once, albeit in a pre-season friendly when Leeds lost to our Merseyside rivals Liverpool in the Charity Shield a few years earlier.

Like all football mad kids, I recalled great FA Cup finals. Growing up in the fifties, I was too young to see the 'Matthews' final in 1953. This was when Stan Matthews helped Blackpool come from behind to defeat Bolton 4–3. I was also too young in 1956 when keeper Bert Trautmann hit the headlines by playing with a broken neck for Manchester City as they overcame Birmingham City. I was old enough to see the great Tottenham Hotspur side claim the double in 1961 while Denis Law starred for Manchester United two years later. Spinning in the six-yard box, Denis stuck it past Leicester City keeper Gordon Banks. I thought, 'Wow!' Of course I was at the Twin Towers when England defeated West Germany in 1966. Running around Wembley was a dream and I hoped that I'd get my opportunity with Everton.

The third round draw was always a much-anticipated occasion and we were satisfied with a home tie against Stoke City, though it would be tough. Coming into the Stoke match there were strong rumours that Billy Bingham would be sacked. The gossip surprised me and did not make sense because he had just spent over £400,000 on players. Billy had joked about a manager being sacked and incredibly it happened in spite of us winning 2–0, courtesy of goals by Mick Lyons and myself. We were delighted to be through to round four, but it was not enough to save Billy. Just 48 hours after the Stoke win, Billy was fired. It was a predetermined decision. Hearing news of the sacking on the radio was a real shock and naturally I wondered how it might affect my future Everton career as Billy had signed me. Bruce and I had played just five games for the boss so it was an uncertain time.

Incredibly, this was the third time in my career that a manager had been sacked shortly after I joined a club. Firstly, Johnny Carey (Nottingham Forest) had been chopped, then Brian Clough (Leeds) and now Billy Bingham. Everton vice-chairman John Moores spoke to the players at Bellefield and informed us that Steve Burtenshaw would take up the role of caretaker-manager until a full time appointment was made. There was massive speculation with big name managers in the frame including England boss Don Revie, Jimmy Armfield (Leeds United), Bobby Robson (Ipswich Town) and Ron Saunders (Aston Villa). There was even talk of former Liverpool boss Bill Shankly coming out of retirement.

Our league form was poor and we were flirting with relegation. Further defeats at Ipswich and at home to Queens Park Rangers didn't help matters, but our cup form was good and next up was a trip to Swindon Town. I was also back on song. I notched a goal in a 3–1 defeat to Rangers as well as further strikes during a 1–1 draw with Bolton Wanderers in a League Cup semi-final clash at Goodison and 2–2 draw at Swindon in the FA Cup. My confidence was returning but it would soon be shattered by news that Gordon Lee was the new Everton manager.

My Everton career appeared doomed before I'd even kicked a ball in anger for the new boss. I'd not spoken to the former Newcastle United manager when I received a phone call from Elton Welsby asking me if I'd seen a Sunday headline in one of the papers. It screamed out 'Where To Next McKenzie?' At first, I thought Elton was winding me up, but he told me to pick up a copy. The headline was bad but the story was worse as it intimated that footballers like Duncan McKenzie were not Lee-type players. Lee was an advocate of team players, not so-called mavericks. I was stunned. It appeared I would be financing a new era under Lee, but I also knew how the newspaper hacks worked. Lee's thoughts may have been taken out of context but even so, I felt decidedly uncomfortable that Sunday afternoon.

Gordon Lee was known as something of a trouble-shooter. Since becoming a manager he had led Port Vale and Blackburn Rovers to promotion from Division 3 and Division 2 prior to becoming Newcastle manager where he took them into Europe and a League Cup final. He had staggered supporters by selling Geordie legend Malcolm Macdonald to Arsenal. SuperMac, a fearsome centre-forward, was outspoken but he did his talking on the park with a stack of goals. Whilst at Newcastle, journalists pushed Lee on Macdonald, which annoyed him, as he wanted to eulogise about the team not so-called superstars. Now at Everton, questions immediately surrounded my future before I'd had a chance to make a real impact.

The new manager was at the helm when we overcame Swindon 2–1 at Goodison to book a fifth round clash with Cardiff City and I had an uneasy feeling. All doubts, though, had to be set aside. I had to knuckle down and try to impress the new boss. Unfortunately results were not going our way as we suffered further league defeats to Aston Villa and Leicester City. Fortunately, our cup exploits brought resilience and Bob Latchford struck the only goal at Bolton to book our Wembley place against Aston Villa. Martin Dobson ended our barren league form with the winner at Stoke before I notched an FA Cup winner to overcome Cardiff City 2–1 although I'd also missed a sitter in the Ninian Park encounter.

Reaching Wembley was a big deal for footballers. For me,

playing in a major domestic English final was massive. I'd sat on the bench in a European Cup final, claimed a Super Cup winner's medal and now I did not want to miss out against Villa. Our dressing room was buoyant after the Bolton match but the win at Burden Park should have been easier as I wasted an excellent opportunity after Bob gave us the lead. Bolton stopper Sam Allardyce booted me up in the air for a stonewall penalty. Big Sam must have thought I'd score so his response was to flatten me in my tracks. Bolton keeper Seamus MacDonald stood so far to one side I thought, 'What is he doing?' but his kidology won. Instead of going bang into the corner, I tried to be clever and put it to the other side but screwed the ball wide. We hung on reasonably comfortably to reach Wembley so my penalty miss did not matter in the end and offered a crumb of comfort for Bolton fans. Both games attracted 50,000 plus attendances.

Three wins in 10 days were just what the lads needed but the Ninian Park dressing room at Cardiff was not a happy one for me as I did not see eye to eye with the new manager over my goal and we had a bust up. The pitch was horrific, resembling a quagmire but as a striker, I always backed myself in difficult conditions and had the legs on my opposite number if he was a big lumbering centreback. With the match delicately poised, I had pinched the ball on halfway and run across my marker's heels. He failed to react and stumbled so I was away. Facing a keeper one-on-one, my policy was always to try to sidestep unless it was obvious I could knock it past him. I shimmied both ways but the Cardiff keeper matched me. I thought to myself . . . you're a better defender than your defenders. I had the ball for what seemed an eternity as four defenders evaded challenging me and ran back to stand on the line. I eventually shimmied around the keeper to face the defenders. For fans, it must have resembled table football. When I shimmied one direction, they moved in synch. I ended up miss-hitting the ball through the legs of a defender for the winning goal. My initial feeling was pure relief. I thought, 'Thank God for that.'

At the final whistle, all the lads were elated. Any win in the cup is terrific and for me any goal, no matter how it goes in, especially in a cup-tie, is terrific. But there was no pat on the back from Lee, who moaned to me 'Why didn't you chuffing hit it?' I couldn't believe the remark and said that I bet he'd rather me hit the ball first time over the bar. We were so far apart in our opinions it was frightening. I wondered what more I could do. I appreciated a striker should ideally run through and whack it past the keeper but that is not always practical. And certainly if you are talking about a player with dribbling skills you should back him all the way. Clearly we had differences.

Domestically then, and now, the League Cup was the poor relation in terms of standing to the FA Cup, which in turn has lost some of its glamour. That has started to change in recent seasons. While the big guns play reserves in early rounds, apart from Arsenal you don't see Manchester United, Chelsea or Liverpool playing an under-strength team in the final. For other Premiership clubs the League Cup offers the only serious chance of silverware and European football. Survival is paramount because of the money involved but Tottenham Hotspur were delighted to win the League Cup in 2008 and celebrated as if they'd won the Premiership. The big four dominate, so clubs on the next rung are delighted to get a shot at major domestic success. Just look at the FA Cup. Portsmouth ultimately triumphed in 2008 but West Brom, Barnsley and Cardiff City reaching the semi-finals gave the tournament a major boost even though it may be a one off.

Off the field, Steve Burtenshaw was a great champion to all the lads. Steve kept American-style player stats, rating two points for a goal and one for an assist. During a training session, he noted that I was top of the ratings, which boosted my confidence. Wembley was around the corner so it was time to knuckle down. Further wins followed against Arsenal and Bristol City but in our 2–1 victory at Ashton Gate, I picked up a shin injury and needed four stitches. It was touch and go for the final, which was a week away. I was desperate to make my first Wembley final and duly got the go ahead during the week, which was a massive relief. I thought, 'Wembley here I come!'

The League Cup final did not have the razzmatazz or build up of an FA Cup final but having the opportunity to play at the Twin Towers was a special feeling. As for television coverage, modern day supporters would be aghast. There was no Friday, Saturday evening, Sunday, Monday, Tuesday, Wednesday or Thursday night live football. We had *Match of the Day* on BBC, which covered three games while ITV ran a football highlights programme offering local coverage on a Sunday. BBC also had a programme called *Sportsnight* on a Wednesday, which offered midweek highlights action. The League Cup final took place on the Saturday afternoon at 3 p.m., the same as a full league programme with highlights shown on ITV on the Sunday. Only the FA Cup final and England-Scotland Home International clash was broadcast live. Times have certainly changed.

The final against Aston Villa was a game we were really looking forward to and for me it would be a first major domestic cup final. Dennis Mortimer was the driving force behind the Villa team and would lead them to a league title and European Cup success in future years. He was a tremendous midfield player and at the hub of everything good about the side at the time. Andy Gray and Brian Little were more the headliners but Dennis made Villa tick.

There is always a scramble for cup final tickets and this game was no exception. Long lost friends sprung up but that was okay. I expected it and helped out where possible. Regarding media coverage, apart from *Shoot* magazine, which made its weekly edition into a special publication, and local media, the build up was almost non-existent nationally until the weekend. It's certainly not on the scale of today when there is wall-to-wall coverage.

Despite the low-key attention nationally, we were fully focused as we travelled to London on the Thursday to visit Wembley. Walking around the stadium got the butterflies going and the tension began to build. My nerves held in check until we travelled to Wembley on match day and made our way down Wembley Way where we saw all the supporters who had made the journey south.

After changing and loosening up, we lined up in the tunnel, which was the most nerve wracking time. Walking on to the Wembley turf was a magical moment and the goose bumps were tangible. The Wembley roar delivered big time but bizarrely kick off was briefly delayed as a Grenadier Guard lost a spur from the back of his boot. The referee and players had to help find the missing spur, which must be a Wembley first.

Princess Anne was guest of honour and I think she must have been a tad embarrassed as her attire was 'Everton' blue. Whoever informed the Princess Royal about dress code got it badly wrong from a neutral perspective. Princess Anne went down both our line-up and the Villa line-up like a train, barely saying a word, but I was determined to stop her for a natter. Being a cheeky bugger, I had to mention the outfit colour. Princess Anne joked that she would sack her advisor and wished me luck.

Everton went into the match as underdogs with the bookies but we felt confident about defeating Aston Villa. There was a terrific feeling of anticipation alongside nerves at kick off but it was important to keep a lid on things. This was the biggest match of my life. It was important to get into the pace of the match quickly. Unfortunately, the final that had such a big build up was anything but the spectacle predicted. The nearest either side came to scoring was when I knocked the ball past Villa left back John Robson, spotted keeper John Burridge off his line and chipped him but the ball landed on the roof of the net. All these years later that is about the only incident I can recall from the game. It must have been a boring spectacle for neutral fans. The match ended 0–0. Both teams went up the Royal steps, shook hands with Princess Anne almost apologetically and jogged around the stadium on a lap of honour. There was a flat feeling as neither team had performed.

In the modern era, there is always a result with the match decided on penalties, but in the seventies, replays were required until a winner was determined. The replay at Hillsborough four days later was a far better spectacle. The match ended 1–1. Aston Villa were more attack-minded than at Wembley and put us under enormous pressure. Villa opened the scoring after a goalmouth scramble. Roger Kenyon was the unlucky Everton player to score an own goal. But we fought back strongly, though could not find a way through Villa's tight defence until deep into injury time when Bob Latchford scrambled a last ditch goal to equalise. Coming off the pitch, we could sense Villa were shaken and back in the dressing room we felt our name was on the League Cup.

The final was entering a third game for the first time in the competition's history, but a month later when the match took place at Old Trafford I was out of favour with the manager. I missed a 2–0 FA Cup quarter-final win over Derby and what would have been my first taste of a home derby against Liverpool, a match that ended goalless. I refused to speculate when quizzed by journalists but requested a clear the air meeting with the manager. We spoke and Lee offered reassurances that

I'd get a chance.

I duly returned in a 4–0 romp against Tottenham Hotspur but found myself dropped for a clash at West Ham. When asked by fans why I was not playing, the manager made it clear that my goal ratio was not good enough. Looking pragmatically at the situation, I could not disagree with his reasoning but at the time, what Lee failed to realise was supporters backed an entertainer, not just a team player. I was disappointed to be dropped but appreciative to have supporter backing.

Meanwhile, the League Cup final second replay was looming. Everton deserved another crack at the trophy, but for me there would only be heartache as I was not even selected as substitute to try to make an impact late on. I was devastated. Sitting in the press box as a match summariser was a surreal experience. I hoped the lads would win but it was tough not being a part of things having played at Wembley and Hillsborough. In many ways, there was a general lack of enthusiasm in the media. The hype of cup final day had long gone and it was not surprising because the final was shown in highlight form only. For players, though, a cup final is a cup final and we desperately wanted to win.

The match turned out to be a classic that went to extra-time. Bob Latchford and Mick Lyons scored our goals while Villa defender Chris Nicholl scored twice including a strike from 45 yards. Brian Little proved to be the Villa hero, scoring the winning goal in a 3–2 victory. I was devastated for the lads. There is no worse place than a losing cup final dressing room. Everyone was deflated and I did not know where to put myself. Looking back, I still can't understand why I was dropped. I must be the only player to take part in two cup finals and not get a medal. It's certainly one for the trivia book!

8

FA CUP AGONY AND EUROPEAN DELIGHT

My debut season at Goodison had turned sour. Following my heartache at missing out on playing in the final act of the League Cup along with the lads, I had to make sure the campaign did not fizzle out. There was still plenty to play for, especially on the cup front. Goals had dried up for me but no one could knock my efforts in putting my all into a game. The only remedy was to battle away in training and wait for an opportunity. All strikers go through lean patches when nothing seems to go right. I had to be patient and, as is often the case, an injury results in a return to the fold. As I said earlier, players don't wish injuries on teammates but it is part of football and I was brought back into the side when we played Derby County a few days after the cup final defeat to Aston Villa.

I was determined to make the most of my opportunity. Fired up for the occasion, I came up trumps with a goal in a 3–2 win. The Everton faithful let me know exactly how they felt and it was good to hear them cheer my name from the rafters. There is nothing better for a footballer than when the fans are behind them in full voice. My return coincided with a return to form as Everton defeated Norwich City four days before an FA Cup semi-final clash against our Merseyside neighbours Liverpool. What's more I was in the side.

Playing against Liverpool was a match to be relished. And having missed a derby clash already I could not wait. What a baptism of fire. It meant so much to both sets of supporters. Dot's family were Evertonians, but not being from the city I could look at the fixture objectively. All derbies are intense but none more so than Everton-Liverpool, Manchester United-Manchester City, Arsenal-Tottenham Hotspur and Celtic-Rangers.

Speaking to supporters and players alike, they agree that unless you're involved it is impossible to understand. There is so much history. Each is a special occasion, form is irrelevant and friendships are discarded for 90 minutes. I've never been to an Old Firm derby but don't doubt pundits and supporters when they say it's a stunning occasion. But all derbies I've attended generate a fantastic atmosphere whether it's in London for a variety of clashes involving the many clubs that play in the capital, Sheffield and Yorkshire area, Bristol, the North East or the Midlands. And all supporters are passionate. Of course, from personal experience, the Merseyside derby is a wonderful occasion but I am biased. These games mean so much to fans and it's why the game will not break away into a European League.

In Liverpool, every derby clash is massive but this game had even more riding on it. For both sets of fans there was no other topic of discussion and the local media lapped it up. Liverpool boss Bob Paisley had done an amazing job since taking over from Bill Shankly and we knew that the game was going to test us like no other. Losing in the League Cup final had knocked us back but this clash refocused our thoughts and energies. As a footballer, you want to play in big games and FA Cup semi-final day is one of the great ones to be involved in. The FA Cup has a magic of its own so the build up nationally was incredible. Both teams last met in a semi-final in 1971 when Liverpool came from behind to win 2–1. Liverpool were firm favourites but we were confident going into the game at Maine Road.

Liverpool had so many star players who were household names, including Ray Clemence, Phil Neal, Joey Jones, Phil Thompson, Emlyn Hughes, Tommy Smith, Jimmy Case, Steve Heighway, Ray Kennedy, Kevin Keegan, John Toshack and Ian Callaghan. For me, Terry McDermott was the most underrated but key player of the side. Terry was such an unsung hero from midfield. A good lad in the dressing room, Terry got on with the job on the pitch, was influential and scored a stack of goals, many spectacular, from deep runs or long-range strikes from midfield. Terry had a great engine and was an unbelievably fit player.

Another unsung hero when compared to the Anfield legends was a red-headed backup striker called David Fairclough but he is rightly lauded as a folk hero at Anfield. On the after-dinner circuit, I always jest about David, dubbed 'Super Sub' by the media, that he played 153 games for Liverpool in two hours 36 minutes! Of course, that was far from the case but it always gets a laugh. His nickname, though, was richly deserved because David had an incredible knack of making an impact against a tired defence and was a potent weapon that Liverpool profited from on many occasions when Paisley threw him into the fray. The thing about David's goals was that they always seemed to come in crucial matches at pivotal moments and none more so than his strike against St Etienne in a European Cup clash, with Liverpool desperate for a goal. David delivered the knockout blow and Anfield folklore states that the roar could be heard miles away as Super Sub had struck again.

There was plenty of banter between the lads. John Toshack

and I discussed it at length during our *Mack 'n' Tosh* radio show that had launched a few months earlier on local radio. Tommy Smith made a guest appearance and I fired questions at the Liverpool stopper, then quickly wished I hadn't. Tommy had a no-nonsense approach on and off the park. When I noted his reputation in a light-hearted manner, Tommy was not amused. The phone lines were jammed with Liverpool supporters saying he'd sort me out and next day car stickers proclaimed 'Tommy Bites Yer Legs Anywhere'. I'd heard that by-line somewhere before!

Come Saturday, the atmosphere was electric and tickets were the hottest in town. Ticket touts made a killing. By kick off, both sides were raring to go and Tommy wasted no time in letting me know he was around with a bone-crunching tackle. I respected Tommy who, like Norman Hunter and Ron Harris, had more to his game than just tackling ability but I was not intimidated. Tommy was hard as nails but I had speed of thought and pace to burn. I was dubbed a Fancy Dan who would nutmeg opponents for fun given half an opportunity. Tommy quickly knew that he was in a game as I showed him a trick or two. Evertonians lapped it up.

Liverpool opened the scoring with a brilliant chip by Terry McDermott. I equalised from 18 yards after Martin Dobson threaded a pass to me and we began to dominate but could not score. Liverpool had a knack of scoring against the run of play, a sign of a great side, and duly struck when Jimmy Case, who had a thunderbolt shot, edged the Reds ahead with a rare header. But we refused to buckle and got our reward when Bruce Rioch stuck a second equaliser. The game was up for grabs and with a couple of minutes left, I nodded a right wing cross into the path of Bryan Hamilton who beat keeper Ray Clemence. For a moment, we were back at Wembley but our celebrations were cut short by a controversial call from referee Clive Thomas who disallowed the goal. We were devastated.

The match ended as a 2–2 draw but there is no Evertonian to this day who does not believe Everton were robbed of facing Manchester United, who defeated my old club Leeds United in the other semi, at Wembley. Back in the dressing room we felt robbed because there appeared nothing wrong with the goal. Liverpool players would have immediately reacted to an Everton infringement but no Liverpool player protested. All our heads went down. Thomas over the years was renowned for contentious decisions and Everton were on the end of, arguably, his worst. Afterwards he said there had been an infringement but did not go into detail and television replays were inconclusive. Unfortunately, 30 years on, nothing has changed, yet technology is in place that can help. Referees are constantly criticised. I accept refs have a thankless task but the day must come when technology gives officials help because nowadays the financial stakes are too high. Decisions have to be right as the very future of a club can be affected by one bad decision.

I witnessed a number of terrible errors first hand when technology proved otherwise. You only have to look at a tape of the 1975 European Cup final when Allan Clarke was chopped down for a penalty with the score at 0–0. Leeds United went on to lose when a goal would have changed the destiny of the game. I don't condone hooliganism, but sitting in the stands must have been unbearable for Leeds supporters who had been on the wrong end of decisions a number of times. The fan reaction at full time was a direct result of a terrible decision. To Everton supporters' credit, they did not react in the same way following the disallowed goal against Liverpool but that particular decision did not end in a defeat at the time.

Following the semi-final, arguments raged but Thomas'

decision could not be overturned. Thomas was one of those referees who seemed to court controversy and his decisions made the headlines rather than the football-related action by the players. Referees have a hugely responsible task but they must have latitude to play advantage. I played under the charge of Jack Taylor, Gordon Hill and Roger Fitzpatrick who enjoyed tremendous respect from players and supporters. All three spotted potential trouble but could take the heat out of the moment. There was also room for banter without things getting out of hand. Unfortunately, all too often nowadays, referees make headlines more than players do.

We felt really hard done by and had to prepare for the replay a few days later at Maine Road. We were determined but I sensed a different atmosphere in the dressing room. There were no excuses, we tried, but when Liverpool were awarded a penalty following an infringement by Mike Pejic on former Everton player David Johnson, we faced an uphill task. Phil Neal scored and Liverpool went on to win 3–0. We were distraught afterwards in the dressing room. Emotions were raw and it took some time to get over the disappointment.

In hindsight, the decision by Thomas knocked the stuffing out of us in the first match. His split second ruling effectively settled the match, as we were not mentally right for the replay. Liverpool were a great side that went on to lose the final against Manchester United but claimed the League title and became the first English club to win the European Cup. This was hard to take for true Evertonians, but as players we had to set aside differences and acknowledge the feat (something that was easier for me as I was not a Scouser). Everton were a big club in their own right with massive support, but Liverpool were European champions for the first time and had set the benchmark other clubs had to match.

It was devastating to miss a second Wembley trip for the biggest domestic final of all, but we had turned around a season from relegation into one of excitement. Although I'd had my differences with the manager, Gordon Lee must take credit for helping us back on the road to recovery. Bar a couple of games out for injury, I played in the remaining fixtures, winning two and drawing five matches as we made up for all the games lost due to the cup runs. We ended the season ninth and it was pleasing to score in the final game at home as Newcastle were dispatched 2–0. The atmosphere was flat, which reflected the way the season had ebbed away. The second half of the season had seen us lose just two matches from 18 games, which showed the impact Lee had made since joining the club. We were effective rather than electrifying but it had brought stability.

I finished the campaign with 10 goals in 26 appearances but there was a sense I'd missed out during a key period of the season. Bob Latchford finished top scorer with 25 goals, so as a partnership things were looking up if we were given the opportunity to start the season together. I still felt uneasy because it was clear I was still not a Lee-type player, but went into the close season determined to get a good pre-season behind me and be raring to go.

Everton had a competitive side worth over £1.5million going into the 1977–78 campaign, which back in the late seventies was a huge sum. Goalkeeper George Wood joined Everton from Blackpool. The best keeper in Division 2, after a shaky start, George developed into a reliable stopper. In defence, we had three stalwarts in Terry Darracott, Mick Lyons and Roger Kenyon. The trio were Everton through and through. Terry overcame barracking to cement a place in the side while Mick and Roger started as apprentices and remained committed through good and bad times. Mick was a stalwart in the heart of defence and filled in as an emergency striker with good effect at times. Before a game, he could not sit still. Mick was perpetual motion. Mike Pejic, a recent transfer from Stoke City, was a hard player who gave opponents a torrid time. A fine left back, no right-winger enjoyed playing against him.

Martin Dobson was the midfield general and key player of the team. A sophisticated footballer and £300,000 capture from Burnley, Martin was a quiet lad in the dressing room but did his talking on the park. Dobbo was the guy you'd give the ball to if you were in trouble to hold it up for you. A very elegant player, he deservedly went on to represent England. Bruce Rioch was a Scottish international and another great midfielder to have in the side. Bruce could handle himself and packed a terrific strike that brought many spectacular goals.

Andy King was a bargain at £35,000 from Luton Town. An aggressive midfielder with an eye for goal, Andy notched his share. Mick Buckley was unfortunate following the Ball-Harvey-Kendall partnership, but contributed when in the side, while Trevor Ross, a £160,000 signing from Arsenal, was a natural ball winner and added balance to the side.

On the wing Dave Thomas supplied the crosses for the strikers. An out and out winger, Dave joined from Queens Park Rangers for £175,000 pre-season. An England international, with trademark socks rolled down, Dave was a graceful player and crowd pleaser, supplying pinpoint crosses from the wing. In my era, genuine out and out wingers were a dying breed. Leeds' Eddie Gray was the best I played against in his pomp while Dave carried the winger's flag in the late seventies and was a throwback to the great Stanley Matthews.

In attack, Jim Pearson signed for £100,000 from St Johnstone and was my main competitor for a first team slot. When one of us was injured, the other got an opportunity. I always believed that if selected, I offered more danger but the boss kept us on our toes by giving us both a run. Leading the line was Bob Latchford. A leading striker in Division 1, Bob led Everton's scoring charts for three seasons before my arrival. Well built, Bob was a terrific target man to partner. Easy going off the park, Bob, at the time, was in dispute with Everton over his contract and wanted a transfer but ever the professional, gave his all in every game.

The lads were great mates and we had a terrific team spirit. On the social side, skipper Mick Lyons liked the lads to mix but there were two camps when it came to drinking. Shortly after joining Everton, Mick asked me to join a few of the Scousers for a drink. I went but soon discovered this merry band liked a good drink on a night, which was way out of my league. Mick and the lads were true Blue to the core and real characters but my definition of going out for a drink was light years apart from theirs, as I'd have ended up going home on a stretcher!

For all the boozing that went on, players of my generation ran it off next day. Mick was typical as he was first in next day for training and would be leading the lads around the training ground while we'd be yelling for him to slow down. Mick had a phenomenal constitution but was also a fantastic player, giving his all in every game. Supporters loved his attitude as a footballer and it was a privilege to play alongside him. I enjoyed a drink with Bruce Rioch, Martin Dobson and Bob Latchford but we were amateurs in the drinking stakes compared to the Scousers. More importantly, the drinking demarcation never split the dressing room.

A drink culture was common at every club in the British game, it's been well documented, and there are plenty of tales on the after-dinner circuit. At Nottingham Forest, I steered away from a night out with Jim Baxter and the drinking lads, while at

Leeds and Everton, Billy Bremner and Mick were leaders of the boozing pack respectively. It was more of a sobering atmosphere when I played for Anderlecht where players went out for a social glass of wine with a meal rather than a booze up, which suited me down to the ground. As a professional footballer, I could never understand why footballers endeavoured to become football maestros on the pitch and drinking legends off it. In the modern game, with the lifestyle influence of foreign players and managers, I'm delighted to see the drink culture is, in the main, deemed off limits.

The beauty of playing on Merseyside, whether a Liverpool or Everton player, was that after playing there was no animosity because all players were part of something very special. The banter is still great when the lads meet up on the after-dinner circuit. As for the fans, of course, it's tribal and more often than not families have mixed support, but Scousers have a wonderful sense of humour, have an ability to laugh at themselves and for me are the most charitable people in Britain.

Playing for a Merseyside giant brought opportunities to help locally in community projects and I was privileged to lend a hand. One project was a five-a-side league for unemployed people, which also involved Liverpool star Steve Heighway. We were seen as sensible lads and went to the no-go areas in Toxteth where police were not particularly welcome. Participants from the area welcomed us as heroes but neither of us viewed it that way. We were delighted just to be involved and hoped it made a difference.

Pre-season training is hard graft and during my time at Everton, a somewhat surprising visitor had the lads in good spirits—none other than former Liverpool boss Bill Shankly. Shanks retired the month I joined Leeds United and likened it to going to the electric chair at the time! Bill later admitted that he resigned too early and at first watched training sessions at Melwood but his presence was unsettling for new manager Bob Paisley.

It's a shame there was no media outlet because Bill would have made a fantastic pundit. Ratings would have been sky high despite his bias to his beloved Liverpool and Liverpool reserves. Football was his life and Everton benefited because his house overlooked Bellefield so he used to pop in and watch us train. Bill was made welcome and he was soon regaling stories to all the lads, including the apprentices who would race to make him a pot of tea.

Bill was so sharp and ready to offer advice at a moment's notice. One day, Terry Darracott arrived at training bleary eyed after a night out on the razz. 'Morning Bill,' he said.

Shanks replied, 'Morning son, how are you?'

Terry said, 'Fine Bill, no problems.'

Shanks, razor sharp as ever, snapped back, 'No problems, what do you mean, son? You've got problems and I've got problems. It's when you've got no problems that you have your biggest problem.'

It was all tongue in cheek and the lads lapped it up. The crack was fantastic. On another occasion, we went training on Formby beach. On our return, Bill asked where we'd been as we did not turn up for training. When Shanks heard, quick as a flash and straight off the cuff he yelled, 'Jesus Christ you don't ask a snooker player to train in a swimming pool. When you play on sand then train on sand.' Shanks was horrified and muttered, 'Total rubbish, total rubbish.' The lads loved him. Bob Paisley rewrote the record books at Anfield but Shanks will always be special at Liverpool.

People say the game in the modern era has lost its characters and in some ways that is true but the likes of Shanks and

Cloughie came from a magical era when managerial characters were aplenty with the likes of Jock Stein, Malcolm Allison and Tommy Docherty. Hacks were provided with plenty of headlines. I'd have loved Shanks, Cloughie and Allison to have been regulars on the circuit but the industry was only just in its infancy then. Fortunately Tommy Doc has been successful and always has an opinion on football on the circuit today.

Thankfully, I did hear Shanks speak with former Manchester City boss Joe Mercer on one occasion when I was in my Nottingham Forest days. I was on a table with Shanks' driver, who drove him from Liverpool to the event and Shanks was sensational. Bill introduced Joe and recalled a game when Scotland played England at Hampden Park in a wartime clash in 1942. Shanks recalled that the score was 4–4 when he tried a speculative long-range shot in the final minute. Recounting the incident, he said ' . . . The great Willie Waddell and Billy Liddell had shown the way with sparkling wing play when I picked the ball up and struck it from deep. The keeper misjudged the bounce and we'd secured a famous 5–4 win. Stanley Matthews, Tommy Lawton, who scored a hat-trick, and Jimmy Hagan were crestfallen as the great Joe Mercer walked off the pitch. Joe knew his team was soundly beaten. I thought to myself at the time, what a sensible man that Joe is because he knew that I'd score.' Shanks' inimitable style was so serious and he had so much belief in his ability. Guests lapped it up.

Like many players I wished I'd had the opportunity to play for Shanks but it never materialised. We did chat about it when he came in for an interview on *Mac 'n' Tosh*. Sitting in the lounge beforehand having a cup of tea, Shanks said, 'Son I made a big mistake when I took Keegan from Scunthorpe because I could also have signed you from Nottingham Forest for £12,000. It was a big mistake. I should have taken the pair of you. If you had come to me then you'd have received education the Liverpool way. You'd have won 100 England caps and been the leading scorer of all time.' Shanks was being pure Shanks but he made me feel 10 feet tall. When I told Tosh he laughed. Shanks told everyone that tale! It illustrates just how he made players feel. As a motivator, Shanks was top notch. Asked whether football was a matter of life or death, Shanks quipped that it was more important, which epitomised everything he stood for. Shanks passed away many years ago but his legend will last as long as people discuss Liverpool FC.

Inconsistency had affected Everton in recent seasons, yet on their day they could match anyone. Evertonians were patient, but Liverpool's dominance frustrated them. Although Everton's inconsistency affected attendances, come the big matches, Goodison was packed and generated an amazing atmosphere. Everton were viewed as a big club but not one of the big four and nothing has changed. Loyal supporters are desperate for success, however, and current boss David Moyes is building a team capable of cementing itself in the top six and challenging for honours. I was delighted to see them reach the FA Cup final last season when the run included a memorable win over Liverpool. Everton fans not only expect attractive football but also a never-say-die spirit.

The lads were refreshed at the start of the 1977–78 campaign. Our cup exploits had given us confidence and after losing our opening two games to newly promoted pacesetters Nottingham Forest (managed by new boss Brian Clough) and Arsenal, we got off to a flyer, remaining unbeaten for 18 matches until Christmas. The loss at Arsenal brought criticism by television pundit and former Liverpool legend Ian St John. His comments niggled me but working in the media, I realised that Saint needed to be controversial and no doubt his points were partly down to the rivalry between Liverpool and Everton. The lads got on with the game and 11 wins in an impressive 18-match run suddenly made opponents, Saint and supporters look at Everton in a different light. Saint even had to eat humble pie briefly.

I was delighted with a run of goals in the opening games. Everton were riding high and pundits predicted my return to the England fold. I struck both goals in a 2–1 win against Aston Villa before hitting the target in victories against Leicester City and Norwich City prior to a strike earning a point at West Ham. A goal in a 3–1 win against West Brom kept the momentum going but unfortunately, I was forced to drop out of the side with a foot injury sustained in a five-goal romp at Queens Park Rangers. Bob Latchford grabbed the headlines, notching four goals, but for me the win was marred as an X-ray revealed a broken bone.

Jim Pearson came into the fray and did a great job. The team continued a fine run until the festive games so there was no way the manager could change the side. But Jim unexpectedly picked up an injury and I was back in the line-up. My return coincided with the team's desperation to bounce back from a 6–2 Boxing Day thumping against Manchester United. On form United were a match for anyone. With an attacking philosophy, wingers Steve Coppell and Gordon Hill continually produced the goods with Stuart Pearson leading the line. In defence, skipper Martin Buchan was difficult to play against because he marshalled opponents well. At times it was like taking on a non-tackling centre half, yet he captained his club and country. Martin had quick feet and formed a great combination with Brian Greenhoff. We went on to lose at Leeds before defeating Arsenal 2–0 on New Year's Eve.

Come January we were challenging in the league and League Cup and looked forward to an FA Cup third round clash against Aston Villa. The lads were determined to avenge our

League Cup final defeat. In a terrific display, we thumped Villa 4–1 and followed it up by edging a league clash with an Andy King goal. The results were pleasing but did not take away the memories of the aftermath at Old Trafford. In a bizarre twist, Clive Thomas officiated the FA Cup clash. He received unbelievable stick from Everton supporters who felt robbed by his decision in the semi-final against Liverpool the previous season. Our win over Villa saw Thomas award us a penalty when I was fouled. Our fans gave him an ironical cheer.

I struck in the FA Cup win over Aston Villa, which sent us to Leeds United in confident mood for a League Cup quarter-final clash, but after taking an early lead, we lost 4–1. Two years down the line from my time at Elland Road, the side I faced was a very different line-up. Jimmy Armfield had rebuilt the Revie team. One path to Wembley had gone and another quickly disappeared when Middlesbrough knocked us out of the FA Cup but our league form was terrific. Bob Latchford was on fire and scoring goals for fun. Bob was looking for 30 league goals in a Division 1 season, which would make him the first player in a decade to do this. An added incentive saw sponsors slap a £10,000 tag, a small fortune in 1978, for the scoring feat.

As a partnership, we'd settled down and combined well over the Easter fixtures as we racked up wins over Newcastle, Leeds, Manchester United and Derby. I struck in the opening two fixtures while Bob hit the target in all four games. The crowds were flocking back to Goodison but there was talk in the football gossip columns that I was on my way out of the club. Rumour had it that Lee wanted to sign Mickey Walsh from Blackpool. After training, he confirmed the news to me. I could not believe it. I told him that if he was going to replace me then he should sign Trevor Francis from Birmingham City rather than Walsh. Francis was clearly going to be a top player. Evertonians, in my view, would slaughter poor Walsh. Micky had scored goals but the decision seemed to be based on his Goal of the Season on *Match of the Day* back in the 1974–75 against Sunderland, which seemed crazy. In the end, a deal fell through but the writing was on the wall for me as the business end of the season approached.

Everton were in the mix with Liverpool, Manchester City and Arsenal to catch leaders Nottingham Forest, who defeated Liverpool in the League Cup final. Brian Clough had resurrected a struggling Division 2 outfit, a far cry from his stint at Leeds. With six games remaining, we were only a few points adrift. Everton were enjoying their best league campaign in years and Evertonians lapped it up.

From being nowhere 12 months earlier, we were now title outsiders as Forest had to slip up to be caught. After defeating Derby County, we faced crunch matches at home to Liverpool and away to Coventry City. Defeats ended our title challenge. We felt down but determined to finish in the top three and qualify for the UEFA Cup. This, of course, was in the days before the Champions League so only the champs entered the premier European competition. The Champions League is a great spectacle but when a fourth placed team can win the accolade of being Europe's top side it does devalue the competition. The true test is for champions only to take part but that will never happen as too much TV money is involved and the latter stages provide great television.

Bob Latchford struck against Ipswich Town but our victory was marred for me as an injury ruled me out for the remainder of the season. A draw at Middlesbrough came on a day when Forest clinched the title at Coventry. Cloughie had pulled off a masterstroke and cemented his place in Forest club folklore by leading the club to a first Division 1 crown. On a national scale he was also on top, having become the first manager since the great Herbert Chapman to win titles with two clubs. Keeper Peter Shilton, who joined the club a few weeks into the season, and my old mate John Robertson were key players to a deserved title success.

At Everton, we focussed on making it into Europe and achieved our goal with two games to go. Bob was on 28 goals but a defeat at West Brom brought only frustration as the 30-goal mark seemed to be slipping away. It was down to the final game at home to Chelsea. I joined a packed crowd with only one thing in mind and that was to cheer him on to the record. As a team, we wanted the big man to do it.

On an afternoon of high drama, we scored twice in the opening 15 minutes through Martin Dobson and Billy Wright. Shortly after half time, Neil Robinson added a third before Bob grabbed number four with 20 minutes to go. The crowd was in raptures and soon it was 5–0 when Mick Lyons scored, but there was unfinished business. Ten minutes from time Chelsea stopper Micky Droy upended Mick for a penalty. Chelsea players were outraged as they did not want a drubbing. There was only one person to take the spot kick. Bob stepped up and blasted the ball past Peter Bonetti for goal number 30, which coincided with the 50th anniversary of Dixie Dean's record-breaking 60 goals in a season. A 6–0 win was the perfect end to the season.

Division 1 leading scorers with 76 goals, we finished third, our best position since winning the league title at the beginning of the decade. Everton would be playing in Europe, which was something to look forward to as players want to test themselves against different opposition. For Evertonians it was a case of Europe here we come, but I knew that I would probably not be part of the campaign. There would be some hard thinking and talking to do over my future during the close season as my football journey was set to take another detour.

9

END OF A FOOTBALLING ODYSSEY

As I anticipated, the approach to the 1978–79 campaign was decision time for me at Everton. I'd had my difficulties with Gordon Lee but overall remained a regular in the side. I'd finished second top scorer with 11 goals the previous season and Evertonians accepted me as a key player in the Everton line-up, which meant a lot to me. Liverpool striker David Johnson was an opponent but also a mate. Chatting one day, David summed up what I brought to the side. Liverpool fans appreciated my talent to such an extent that when a Brazilian kid saw David doing tricks with the ball, the youngster yelled out, 'Hey it's Duncan McKenzie!' This was great for my confidence but reality was setting in at Goodison.

I gave my all during pre-season training but was out of the frame when we kicked off the campaign with an 8–0 thumping of Wimbledon in the League Cup. Bob Latchford carried on where he left off the previous season by banging in five goals while Martin Dobson notched a hat-trick. In the league, Everton made their best start since winning the league in 1969–70 with wins over Chelsea, Derby County and Arsenal but I was not in the starting line-up. Everton would enjoy a 19-match unbeaten run en route to a fourth placed finish but my days at Goodison were well and truly numbered. It was time to move on.

Although I rated the set up and loved playing for Everton, I had to face facts that Lee wanted me out. And the writing had been on the wall arguably since his arrival. I had a contract and could have stuck it out, but Mickey Walsh from Blackpool was about to arrive and I didn't want to be kicking about playing reserve team football. In a clear the air chat with the manager, I realised that I'd not figure even if Walsh were injured. I told Lee I'd move on when the right deal came up. At 28 I was not finished and believed that I could still hack it in the top flight. I was still confident in my ability to knock in a few goals. Goal scoring never leaves a striker, even if a yard of pace and sharpness wanes a tad. I had a number of offers from interested clubs but Chelsea and Middlesbrough were the leading teams showing interest.

A deal at Boro never materialised and I knew there was turmoil at Stamford Bridge. But Chelsea offered me the same money I was on at Everton. I thought to myself, 'I'm not wanted at Everton, give it a go.' I was allowed to train at Wigan, which was commutable from where I lived, and travelled down the night before matches. The package suited me. A few years earlier I'd promised Bill Nicholson at Tottenham that I would not play for another London club but he'd departed from White Hart Lane so morally I felt okay. I also knew that this was just a stopgap move on the road to retirement from the game that had given me a fantastic lifestyle.

Chelsea had endured tough times since the heady days of the swinging sixties and early seventies under skipper Ron Harris when Chelsea won the FA Cup and European Cup Winners Cup. During my early years at Nottingham Forest I admired the likes of Peter Bonetti, Peter Osgood, Alan Hudson, Ian

Hutchinson, Charlie Cooke and David Webb but the club had suffered since many of the stars of that side had peaked. Relegated in 1974–75, financial problems meant the club had sold the training ground but they had bounced back inside two seasons. 'Chopper' Harris was still making life a misery for attackers and 'The Cat' Bonetti was still between the sticks, however both were coming to the end of stalwart careers and it must have hurt them to see the club struggling.

On the bright side, there was a pool of talented youngsters in Tommy Langley, Ray Wilkins, Kenny Swain, Ian Britton and Steve Wicks but it was a different era at The Bridge. Chelsea supporters, as always, were vociferous in support, even if there was a minority element hell bent on causing trouble off the pitch. But I was determined to entertain and make an impact. Ken Shellito was manager. Ken, a fine coach, had been promoted to the hot seat the previous season when Chelsea were trying to re-establish themselves among the elite. I joined alongside Eamonn Bannon (Hearts) and Petar Borota (Partizan Belgrade). Petar was seen as a replacement for Bonetti, who had over 700 appearances to his name.

It did not take long to see that the club was in a mess. Off the field wrangling had manifested itself with pitiful displays on the pitch. The team had plenty of spirit but limited ability. The writing was on the wall from the start. Oh, what Chelsea could have done with Roman Abramovich at the helm back in 1978. I'd joined a club on the slide with just a solitary win at Wolves to show from the opening four games. I made a scoring debut in a 3–2 defeat at Coventry City and notched an equalising goal at Birmingham but losing appeared the norm. Chelsea fans had something to cheer when we edged a thrilling encounter at home to Bolton 4–3, a match I missed through injury. It would be the last victory for three months as a long winter set in for Blues fans.

I was back in the side when we battled hard before losing at Anfield and following hard-earned points in a 3–3 thriller against Norwich and scoreless draw against West London neighbours Queens Park Rangers, I faced my former club Everton. It was a strange feeling going back to Goodison but desperate for points, I wanted to impress and enjoyed a fair old game. When I ran on to the park, I was given a terrific welcome but even I did not expect the ovation that came my way from home supporters when I fired home the first goal of the match. We lost 3–2 but supporters, who mention it from time to time when I'm at a home game, did not forget my strike for Chelsea. And neither have some of my former teammates.

I always enjoy meeting the lads to catch up on what has been happening during the intervening years and to reminisce about the good old days. Occasionally I glean insights into what some of them thought of me as a player. A great pal and exceptional footballer, Martin Dobson demonstrated this very fact during a Question and Answer session with Everton fans a few years ago. Martin took me completely by surprise.

Question and Answer sessions are always enjoyable as there is a mix of players from different eras so interrogation by supporters is guaranteed to be lively and informative. During such a session, a supporter asked Martin about his favourite Everton players and my name cropped up for a variety of reasons including my Chelsea goal at Goodison Park. Martin could not believe the applause I received from the Everton faithful. They went absolutely berserk as if their favourite player had scored the winning goal for the home team. The Evertonian reaction had stayed with Martin for 20 plus years because he'd never witnessed anything like it as a professional footballer. Martin went on to explain that he fully understood the fan reaction because players of my ilk played with a smile at all times.

Perceptions are interesting because when I look back over my career, sometimes I wish that I were more like the player Martin was describing. It's crazy but even though I consciously wanted to entertain, I genuinely felt that at times I was a little too serious. Yet Martin believed my attitude was always to entertain fans.

Sadly our defeat to Everton was one of many during a dreadful spell of results and soon a new manager was at the helm when Ken departed before Christmas. Ken Shellito was a true Blue. A junior at Chelsea, over 12 years as a professional, his playing career was dogged by injury but Ken's true asset was nurturing young players. A well-respected youth team coach, Ken was promoted to a job that did not suit him. Initially club chairman Brian Mears wanted to appoint a big hitter in Yugoslavia coach Miljan Miljanic but negotiations faltered. Mears appointed right-hand man Frank Upton as caretaker-boss.

Frank was a nice guy who was only in place to hold the fort, which didn't last long. Frank came into the dressing room as we changed for training on his first day at the helm. He told the lads that while he was in charge there would be no nonsense calling him by his first name, as had been the norm. Players should call him boss. Peter Osgood, quick as a flash quipped, 'What's that Frank?' Naturally, Frank was not happy. Peter looked at him with a cheeky glint in his eyes. There was no way that Frank could win, Peter had his number. Three hours later Mears called a meeting to tell us former Tottenham great Danny Blanchflower, now a renowned journalist, had stepped in on a month-to-month basis as manager. We waited to meet Danny but before he arrived, Frank stuck his head around the corner of the door and informed Peter that it was okay to call him Frank again. We all cracked up!

Life at the Bridge could, at best, be described as farcical.

The managerial shenanigans were crazy while on the field we continued to struggle. There was no festive cheer for Chelsea supporters as Middlesbrough hammered us 7–2 and Ipswich romped to a 5–1 win. Goalless draws with struggling Bristol City and Southampton separated the defeats, but fortunately I missed participating in the debacle of both thumpings, though I watched aghast as we fell apart. Our dressing room was not a happy place. The Middlesbrough match, in particular, was a joke. Before the game Osgood, God bless him, had returned to the club to help out in the looming crisis and tried to organise tactics with Brian Harris and the new boss, but it was like working with Tweedledee and Tweedledum. Discipline was shot.

Manchester United mercifully knocked us out of the FA Cup with a routine victory and I made just one more appearance for Chelsea, scoring our second goal in a 3–2 win over their neighbours Manchester City. My stay would prove shorter than either Chelsea or I planned and what kept me sane was staying with good friends when I was not commuting. I was not surprised that a tortuous campaign ended in relegation for Chelsea who claimed just five wins and conceded almost a century of goals, the largest total by some distance in the league. It was a season to forget for Blues fans. Chelsea claimed just 20 points, which was the lowest in the club's history. A theorist more than a taskmaster, Blanchflower lacked a ruthless approach to cut it as a manager and left as Chelsea searched for former glories.

Modern day Chelsea has become a crack outfit since the arrival of Abramovich. With massive funds available, Jose Mourinho, in particular, took the club to new heights and they are a major force in European football. Mourinho, for me, is the modern day Brian Clough, without the green sweatshirt! Mourinho, like Cloughie, is a great character and Chelsea players loved him until his surprise departure. Jose backed his stars to the hilt, defended them to the hilt and as a result players played for him until they dropped. For the players and the manager it was the perfect partnership.

Former Forest great Kenny Burns is one of my golfing buddies and always speaks highly of Cloughie. All the Forest lads loved him. Brian was a different person in front of the press in comparison with the man behind the scenes. Cloughie was great for the game, like Mourinho is now. It was a great shame when Mourinho parted company with Chelsea but Abramovich bank rolls the club and clearly makes the tough calls. Jose has achieved at every club he has managed and I'm sure his current club Inter Milan will benefit. You can be sure Inter will be challenging for honours.

History has a habit of repeating itself with characters such as Clough and Mourinho. It was demonstrated when the Leeds board replaced Brian with a steady hand in Jimmy Armfield and Chelsea did the same when Mourinho was replaced by Avran Grant. Directors for some reason seem to go from one extreme to another. Moving on to last season, Chelsea got it spot on with the appointment of Luiz Felipe Scolari but I was amazed when he was sacked. 'Big Fel' (pronounced Phil) is a winner. He proved it with Brazil and Portugal; he demands and gets total commitment in every game and deals with the media head on. Chelsea fans knew there was no guarantee of success because in football everything has a cycle. Chelsea is an ageing team and no side can dominate forever. If Chelsea were to continue competing at the highest level, they needed to invest big money. Scolari's sacking was an astonishing decision because I'm sure he would have won honours given time and he will no doubt be successful in the future. Guus Hiddink came in as caretaker-boss to steady the ship and guided the team to an FA Cup triumph over Everton to pacify supporters. Current boss Carlo Ancelotti has standing but reputations mean nothing to Abramovitch, so it will be interesting to see how things develop at Stamford Bridge.

Commuting to London had been tough and I realised that joining Chelsea was a mistake. When Blackburn Rovers enquired about my services in March 1979 the opportunity was most welcome. As I drove home, I was looking forward to discussing the move with Dot, but panic stations replaced all thoughts of transfers when I turned the corner into my street and saw an ambulance outside our house. My first thought was Dot. There were no mobile phones in those days so I didn't have a clue there was a major problem at home. Dot was fine, but we had lost a two-week old baby boy through a cot death. Losing a child is something you never get over but learn to live with. It happened in an era when not much research had been done into cot deaths, unlike today. Our son's death was tough to come to terms with for a long time. Consequently, when Riah was born 11 years later, there was total paranoia in the McKenzie household in terms of fitting a baby alarm and so on.

Blackburn approached me at just the right moment. With everything going on at home, there was no way I wanted to be away for long periods. I moved to Ewood Park in a £75,000 club record deal. My big earning days were over, although I appreciated that my salary at Blackburn was large in comparison with other players' salaries. Dropping into the third tier of football did not worry me as Blackburn battled relegation from Division 2. Rovers boss John Pickering made it clear I was at Ewood Park to do a job. I told John that I'd always been a player who wanted to play. John said, 'Great to have you on board, Dunc.'

Blackburn had endured a topsy-turvy decade in Division 2 and 3. My former boss at Everton, Gordon Lee, had guided

them to the Division 3 title in 1974–75 before he joined
Newcastle United and ended my hopes of a long career on
Merseyside. When I arrived at Ewood Park the club was a
shambles and fighting a losing battle against relegation. Team
morale was at an all-time low. Reserve team manager John
Pickering had succeeded Jim Iley as first team boss mid-season
amid rumours of player unrest. Credit to the board, they gave
Jim funds to bring Mick Rathbone (Birmingham City), Dave
Wagstaffe (Blackpool) and myself in to battle away. We would
be playing alongside the likes of promising youngster John Bailey
(who would soon star for Everton), stalwart defenders Derek
Fazackerley (who would go on to break Ronnie Clayton's all-
time appearance record), Glen Keeley and Irish international
Noel Brotherston.

John asked me to play midfield, which was terrific because
I was getting a tad tired of being kicked from pillar to post. The
move gave me a new lease of life. I was involved in the game
more, which suited me. I enjoyed being in the middle of the
park, but even with my new focus and new squad additions,
survival was a tall order. To be fair, the manager was aware of the
situation as Blackburn had won just three games all season. But
credit to John, his changes altered our fortunes as seven victories
came in the final third of the season, which was nothing like
relegation form, but it was too little too late.

On joining the team, my aim was to add a touch of
experience, savvy and to score goals. I managed to notch a couple
including a winner against West Ham but there was too much
ground to make up. Blackburn were doomed and we finished
five points from safety. John had tried his utmost and incredibly
after our final home game, home supporters mobbed the players
for our efforts, which was appreciated. John's efforts, however
commendable, were not given time to develop by the board as

they decided not to renew his contract. The 1978–79 season had been a bizarre one for me. I left a club at the top of Division 1 and played for two sides that were then relegated. No doubt that fact has been a great trivia question in some circles. I'd also played for three managers and two caretaker-bosses. As *Saint and Greavsie* used to say on their pre-match football show on a Saturday lunchtime, 'It's a funny old game'.

By the start of the new season, former Everton legend Howard Kendall, who had helped guide Stoke City to promotion from Division 2 as player-coach, was at the helm as Rovers' first player-manager. The transition from being a player to manager is not easy and does not always work. Howard had enjoyed an excellent career at Everton, the highlight coming when he played alongside Colin Harvey and Alan Ball in the 1970 Division 1 championship side, but this was his first true managerial post. The coming two seasons would make Howard one of the club's most successful managers with back-to-back promotions only denied by goal difference which, on any basis, is a terrific achievement. Howard would be one of the hottest managerial properties and on his way to the top at his beloved Everton.

Before such glories, though, Howard had to search out talent from the lower reaches of the football pyramid or from those struggling to make the first team. Pre-season, he asked me whether I'd return to a striking role, which I was happy to do even though I felt I'd be more effective in midfield. Unfortunately, it did not matter where I played as the new campaign began with a hangover from the previous season as we claimed just one victory, a 3–0 win at Sheffield Wednesday where I notched our last goal, and five draws from the opening 10 games. It was a worrying start.

As we were struggling at the wrong end of the table, unbeknown to me a number of the senior lads including

Fazackerley, Keeley and Tony Parkes had a meeting with the manager to see if he'd push me back into midfield where they felt I'd have more impact. Howard told them about my goal scoring record at other clubs and the fact that I was already leading the scoring charts with five league and cup goals despite our poor form. The lads persisted and felt that I'd still score my share. They explained that I'd played midfield the previous season and had been effective. Howard agreed to give it a go and told me I could have a free role in midfield.

Sometimes it takes players to tell a new manager the strengths of a team, but I knew that Howard was just trying to make his mark and fair play to him. It's a balancing act and good on him as he listened to the players. The tactic paid off. Boosted by the news, a further fillip came with the arrival of Jim Branagan (Huddersfield Town) and Andy Crawford (Derby County). Both were looking for regular first team football and Rovers could supply it. The pair joined Jim Arnold (Stafford Rangers) who arrived during the close season and all proceeded to help us turn the corner with a fantastic run. Our defensive unit of Arnold together with Branagan, Rathbone, Keeley and Fazackerley proved the meanest outside the top flight, shipping just 36 goals in 46 league games, which was some effort. The defensive lads made a massive impact, as we shot up the league during an incredible unbeaten run of 14 wins from 15 matches. I'd played at the highest level in domestic football and in Europe but this three-month period was sensational to be involved in, even if it was at the lower echelons of the league ladder.

During this purple patch I'd also not lost my scoring touch as I struck twice in a 2–1 win at my hometown club Grimsby Town (who led the way at the time) to kick start our promotion drive. The result boosted our confidence. We did not hammer teams—we won seven games by a solitary goal. I got the all-important strike in two of these clashes, at home to Hull City and on an away day at Mansfield Town. On occasions, we did hit three goals and I was delighted to be on target each time as we disposed of Wimbledon, who are slowly battling their way back to league status, Brentford and Gillingham. In all, I hit the target eight times during the 15-match run while Andy Crawford notched seven goals. The team was on fire and following a 2–0 defeat at Exeter City, wins over Reading, Oxford and Bury in the final five games secured second spot by a point, despite our nearest rivals Sheffield Wednesday defeating us in our final home game in front of packed house. Grimsby secured the title by three points.

We enjoyed some terrific results during the season and not just in the league. After I notched two goals in a 3–2 win over Bury in the League Cup we faced European Cup holders Nottingham Forest. I had no feelings of regret as to what might have been had I stayed at the club all those years ago. As a former player I was delighted they had been so successful. Cloughie was in fine form when I bumped into him outside the dressing room prior to the match. Forest showed no mercy as they smashed six past us on the route to a 6–1 win in front of a bumper crowd of over 21,000. That attendance was eclipsed when we embarked on a superb FA Cup run. Andy Crawford provided the knockout blow as we despatched non-league Kidderminster Harriers and Stafford Rangers before causing something of a cup shock by eliminating Division 2 outfit Fulham.

Blackburn was not renowned as a hotbed of football and nothing has changed all these years later. But the FA Cup is a special tournament and cup fever gripped the town. Andy made headlines again as he knocked out top flight Coventry City. I enjoyed one of those days when everything came off. It was a screaming day but our cup adventure would only last until round five when Aston Villa knocked us out after a replay. We drew 1–1 at Ewood Park when just short of 30,000 packed the ground before we went out to a solitary strike at Villa Park. There was no disgrace in our efforts and we received plenty of praise in the press next day.

The crowd for our fifth round clash summed up Blackburn Rovers supporters. I felt for Mark Hughes in recent seasons because it cannot have been easy trying to compete with the best when your ground was rarely full. It was tough and I was not surprised to see him take up the challenge of bringing back the glory days to Manchester City. Blackburn's appointment of Paul Ince was brave and forward thinking. I was disappointed that he was only given a few months at the helm but Sam Allardyce will bring stability. Big Sam is an experienced campaigner and knows what it takes to survive at the top level.

We were not the most entertaining side to watch and our play was like the fans, a bit dour. Blackburn supporters seemed to have a negative attitude. One old bloke used to say to me, 'When you can see Darwin Hill it's a sign of rain and when you can't see it then it's already raining!' Another old-timer told me he had not been to a game since the 1960 Cup Final because they would not give him a cup final ticket. Some fans held long memories.

The campaign had gone well and when promotion was on the cards all the lads were promised a post-season trip to Majorca for a week. But the board of directors were the tightest bunch of directors I've ever come across. When the due trip came there was no players' pool for spending money, so club captain Jimmy Branagan collected a few pounds from each player towards a kitty.

Simon Garner was not only a great goal scorer at this level of

football but also a bit of a rebel. The first night on tour he arrived
back at the hotel worse for drink, singing at the top of his voice
and making a total nuisance of himself. Howard threatened to
send him home the following day and explain to the local press
why he was home early. Simon was on a final warning. We had a
terrific time and at the airport, Howard congratulated Simon for
not causing a nuisance at the hotel after the early incident. Simon
gave him a wry smile and said he was not surprised as he'd slept
on the beach all week to sober up. The lads cracked up.

Promotion meant a happy summer with me contemplating
life in a higher league. The manager strengthened midfield by
signing Mick Speight from Sheffield United and we were
immediately on a roll challenging for promotion. Seven wins in
the opening 10 matches saw us hit the top but we did struggle to
score goals. Howard needed to recruit a striker but was told that
he needed to offload another player. In the world of lower league
football, juggling finances was, and still is, a constant problem.
The Blackburn board could not afford to renew my contract so
I was the obvious candidate to move on. Howard told me that he
did not want to lose me because I added experience. He
described the board decision as a hammer blow but asked me to
do my best while he looked to do his best for me. I understood
his dilemma and waited for news.

I'd enjoyed my spell at Rovers and there were some great
characters in the side. Mickey Rathbone, currently
physiotherapist at Everton, was certainly one. Affectionately
called Basil, Mickey was the whipping boy at the time, as he
played right back while Howard played right half. If anyone went
past Howard, Mickey got the blame if he failed to cover, and if
Mickey did cover the boss and opponent wingers got a cross in,
then he still got the blame. Poor Basil was in a lose-lose situation.

Another incident that made me smile was when Mickey took

throw-ins from his side of the field. Howard was generally the nearest player and liked the ball thrown knee-high to him on his right foot so he could volley it up the park from defensive situations, which was an easy way of not losing the ball in our third of the field. This tactic had gone on for a period of time when suddenly Mickey, no matter how hard he tried to be accurate, continually threw the ball in the wrong place. Howard was not happy. In one game, after around 20 minutes, the linesman gave Blackburn a throw. Mickey told the linesman he'd made the wrong decision as he did not want another berating from the boss. The lads were amused.

My career was soon to take another road because Tulsa Roughnecks of the North American Soccer League (NASL) came in for me as Christmas approached. The opportunity had come about through Cloughie's sidekick Peter Taylor who recommended me to Tulsa. Charlie Mitchell was manager and my old teammate from Forest days, Terry Hennessey, was coach. Terry, who would take over as coach during the 1981 campaign, was chatting to Peter about potential players who may be able to adapt to AstroTurf and recommended me. Peter said, 'Get Duncan McKenzie, he'll be brilliant. Nobody will be able to touch him with his close ball control and speed off the mark even at his age.' I thought, 'Thanks Pete!'

Howard asked if I fancied playing in America. I discussed it with Dot. She said that it would be a great swansong and we'd have a ball. The weather would be fantastic and Tulsa sounded like a wonderful place. Speaking to a number of lads who had played in the US, the lifestyle appeared to be exceptional and it did not take me long to agree. Tulsa was amazing. When you talk about job descriptions, mine was near perfect. Tulsa were to pay me to play football in every major city in North America.

While I waited to make my debut across the Atlantic,

Blackburn enjoyed a fine second half to the season, losing only twice, but six victories and 10 draws would ultimately cost Rovers dearly as Swansea City claimed the last Division 1 promotion spot by a goal difference of just one. The Blackburn board had been short sighted because promotion was on the cards. Howard lamented some time later to me that one of my goals could have made all the difference, but the board could not see beyond the end of its nose. Rovers' rise had alerted Division 1 outfits and Howard could not resist the challenge of replacing Gordon Lee at Everton. It's amazing how my footballing journey crossed paths with Everton and I was delighted to see him succeed at Goodison Park in the mid-eighties as it pleased all Evertonians.

The dream of a professional league in the United States and Canada started in 1966. Administrators hoped slowly to gain a foothold alongside the mainstream sports of American football, baseball and ice hockey. This was a tough ask because these sports had dominated the landscape but by the late seventies crowds of 70,000 were packing Giants Stadium to watch New York Cosmos and its star player Pele. Other high profile world stars at the end of careers opting to take the highroad to the US in a bid to promote the game included Franz Beckenbauer (New York Cosmos), George Best (Los Angeles Aztecs, Fort Lauderdale Strikers and San Jose Earthquakes), Georgia Chinaglia (New York Cosmos), Johan Cruyff (Los Angeles Aztecs and Washington Diplomats), Teofilo Cubillas (Fort Laurderdale Strikers) and Eusebio (Boston Minutemen, Toronto Metros-Croatia and Las Vegas Quicksilver).

Apart from Bestie, who played six seasons in the NASAL, other British players to make a mark were Rodney Marsh playing over five seasons for Tampa Bay Rowdies, Mike England and Alan Hudson playing for a similar period at Seattle Sounders, and Ron Futcher playing for nine seasons at Minnesota Kicks,

Signing for Everton from Anderlecht   ©*Press Association*

Scoring for Everton against The Villa   @*Getty Images/Bob Thomas*

Shooting for goal past United's Arthur Albiston   ©*Getty Images/Bob Thomas*

Ray Clemence briefly replaced John Toshack in the Mac 'n' Tosh radio show
©*Getty Images/Bob Thomas*

Playing for Chelsea and competing for the ball with Paul Power (left) of Manchester City during a First Division match at Stamford Bridge. ©Getty Images/Peter Cade

Being tackled by Coventry City's Bob McDonald in a Chelsea v Coventry match in 1978 ©Getty Images/Bob Thomas

Greeted by Chairman Derrick Keighley (left) and secretary John Haworth (right) when arriving at Ewood Park to sign for Blackburn Rovers ©Howard Talbot

Playing my debut game for Blackburn Rovers against Preston ©Howard Talbot

'Catch me if you can!' Taking on three Huddersfield Town defenders in the first round, first leg Football League Cup tie at Ewood Park ©Howard Talbot

Pre-match with Everton academy at Goodison

Golfing in Tenerife: having a drink with Kevin Keegan and Renato

With Dot and Riah dressed to impress

In cruise gear in the Caribbean

With Johan Cruyff

With the great Sir Norman Wisdom OBE—always a scream on the golf course

Portland Timbers and Tulsa Roughnecks. There was real hype and the game did grow, but the key was to develop local stars. The retirement of Pele in 1977 heralded an eight-year slide to oblivion when the league folded but there was still a demand when my opportunity came along. 'Razzmatazz here I come,' I thought and duly traded places with Viv Busby to join the American footballing bandwagon at Tulsa if only for a brief time.

A lot of English players who had failed to make the grade in Division 1 also made the journey, together with former opponents I'd come up against in top-flight football. There was certainly plenty of talent because they included Brian Kidd (Atlanta Chiefs), Charlie Cooke (California Surf), Phil Parkes (Chicago Sting), Keith Weller (Fort Lauderdale Strikers), Tony Brown (Jacksonville Tea Men), Steve Heighway (Minnesota Kicks), Gordon Hill (Montreal Manic), Frank Worthington (Tampa Bay Rowdies) and Jimmy Greenhoff (Toronto Blizzard).

The league campaign started in the April so there was time to get accustomed to the conditions. History shows that the 1981 season started a real decline in the league as franchise membership dropped from 24 to 20 teams. US franchises Atlanta, Detroit, Houston, Memphis and Rochester folded while New England moved to Jacksonville, Florida and Philadelphia moved to Montreal. Fifteen American teams lined up alongside five Canadian sides, with Calgary Boomers being the newest franchise.

Tulsa played in the Central Division four times against Chicago Sting, Minnesota Kicks and Dallas Tornado. The 32-match season saw us take on a further 10 sides twice. Six points were awarded for a win, plus an additional point for each goal up to a maximum of three per team. Draws were not allowed so a 15-minute sudden death overtime period took place if a match was level after 90 minutes, followed by a shoot-out. Over the season we won three of six games in overtime but lost out in five of six games that went to a shoot-out. My goal scoring knack did not desert me. I quickly got our supporters on my side by scoring an overtime winner against Dallas in my second match and shortly after scored another against Calgary. Further goals helped us defeat Portland, Montreal, Washington and Vancouver.

At the end of the regular season we ultimately lost out in the playoffs to Minnesota. Chicago Sting defeated New York Cosmos in the Soccer Bowl. On the field, I missed one match and was delighted with my strike rate of 14 goals together with 16 assists. My efforts saw me collect the Most Valuable Player (MVP) award at Tulsa and I also finished the season in the top 10 of leading scorers, which was very satisfying. Points were awarded for goals and assists. Chinaglia was the most prolific goal scorer in NASL history and finished top of the charts during the campaign.

Stat recognition is now common in the English game but back in the early eighties it was an alien phenomenon. Obviously American coaches adapted the system from other US sports such as baseball, basketball and American football. What they appreciated was not only the goal scorers but also overall play, which was terrific. It is important for players in a squad to be appreciated and nowadays every club in professional football monitors skill sets. Now you hear about pass completion, tackles made, assists, headers won and so on. But teams still need a goal scorer otherwise they will struggle. Getting recognition was terrific for me because in my playing days in England only Everton coach Steve Burtenshaw caught on to the stat game. Steve tried to impress Gordon Lee but he was only interested in muck and nettle football. That was in the past, though, as I enjoyed the final phase of my professional career.

At Tulsa, gates were around 20,000, which was good by US figures. The standard was decent but unlike in the English game, players had time on the ball. If you could trap and pass like the Europeans and South Americans then you were allowed to play. The American lads were not great players but they were tremendous athletes. Each team had around four Americans in a team supported by foreign imports, some being naturalised Americans.

Tulsa were perennial strugglers so expectations were low. Carl Moore, whose son Joe Max Moore represented the US national team and Everton, owned the club. Carl went out of his way to help me settle, which caused some problems with the US-based players. I needed a car so Carl gave me a Delorean. Naively I didn't realise the feelings of jealousy this generated. Coaches Terry Hennessey and Alan Woodward (who played for Sheffield United in his pomp) were not happy about the benefit. Fortunately I gained respect on the park.

Off the field, I loved the lifestyle but didn't have much luck with my apartment. The first apartment was damaged in a flash flood and suffered fire damage but that was nothing compared to what happened to Alan when a tornado struck. Woody rang me to come over as half the neighbour's house was in his swimming pool! Amazingly nothing else was damaged but that is a tornado. It bounces down, picks something up and dumps it. It was an astonishing sight.

Playing in America suited my game and the pace of life was terrific. I got to see wonderful places and it was five-star all the way. But soccer was not the number one sport and never will be because it's not in the American psyche. In 1994, I covered the World Cup for an American hospitality company. A local reporter covering a game summed up the negative attitude when he moaned about a match that ended in a draw. His attitude was incredible because where the match took place there were more soccer teams than in any other city I'd played in. Okay, many were girls and veteran teams but the sheer number of people playing was phenomenal. Also, kids' summer camps were packed with youngsters playing the sport. The hack may not have liked football but the US have since reached the quarter-finals of the World Cup and don't be surprised if they return to be ranked in the top 10 football-playing countries. Just look at the amount of dollars thrown at the game with the likes of David Beckham going to play soccer there. Soccer may not dominate because it's a closed shop for major sports in terms of US television rights but it can compete on a global level as demonstrated when it took a late goal by Brazil to win the FIFA Confederations Cup final in South Africa last summer.

By the start of the 1982 season I was playing for Chicago Sting. The NASL, like all American sports, worked on a draft system so when struggling Tulsa received four top-rated American-based players I had to move on. Tulsa could play only five overseas players so the quality of Americans determined how well a team did. With players arriving I was surplus to requirements and it was not like in the UK where you sit in the reserves and wait for an opportunity. If a club chose to trade you in the draft system, as in American Football, baseball or basketball, then you had to move otherwise you didn't get paid. Needless to say, it was not a difficult decision. Also, faced with a choice of going to Chicago to continue playing or returning home to retire it was not a tough decision to make.

To me the draft system is not a bad idea as it gives poor teams a chance to compete the following season but it would not work in Europe as it's never been part of the sporting culture. Americans have grown up with the system and have the infrastructure around it. Arguments about limiting foreign players in Europe has raged for years but with freedom of contract there is no way football authorities can implement it and the legal system makes sure of that, though it is to the detriment of the national team. It's a shame as it would bring more competition and it must be soul destroying for young players trying to break into any club. Quotas on foreign stars have worked in other sports such as cricket and would benefit football but it will never happen.

On the field, only 14 teams took part in the 1982 season as Calgary, California, Los Angeles, Minnesota Washington and Dallas Tornado dropped out of the league. Under FIFA pressure the 35-yard offside rule also disappeared. During the campaign I started to pick up injuries and only played 20 games of the regular season. Chicago failed to make the playoffs. New York Cosmos defeated Seattle Sounders in the Super Bowl and Chinaglia again finished the season as top scorer.

Reflecting on my two seasons, the NASL was an important part in the development of soccer in the United States and I was pleased to have played my part before its demise in 1985. Tornados and flash floods aside, I took to the American lifestyle, especially in the country. I loved Oklahoma but not Chicago (Chicago was a great place to spend a weekend, a bit like visiting London). One of the great thrills in Chicago was seeing Yul Bryner 'live' in the hit musical *The King and I*. Despite the fact that Yul was knocking on a bit, puffing and panting after the dance routines, it was still a treat. I could have got a green card when I was at Tulsa and Chicago but for some reason didn't get around to it. Looking back, if I had got a visa sorted out we may have stayed on and who knows what might have been? I'm not one to regret past decisions, though. It was time to return home.

I did think my footballing career was over and was mentally prepared for this when I received a call out of the blue from Ian

St John who had a mate involved with a Hong Kong side called Royden, struggling in the national league. The owners wanted to save face as a big company was backing them. I thought it would be a nice little earner but when I went out the monsoons arrived so all games were cancelled. I stayed in Hong Kong for four months rather than two weeks because Royden did not want to let me leave in case games resumed and were willing to pay me a retainer. I thought 'Okay!' Dot came out for a couple of weeks but it was not going to last. I was ready to hang up my boots. My playing days were over. It was time to join Civvy Street.

10

ENGLAND HEROES, HEARTACHE AND FUTURE GLORY

When I came into the game, the dream was to represent England. Having witnessed the World Cup triumph in 1966 first hand, I desperately wanted to make a mark on the international game but knew it would be a tough ask. I had confidence in my own ability to make a mark and get recognised. During my career I got the chance to train with and face a number of the boys of 1966 and looking back I'm delighted that I did. The players in the England XI that defeated West Germany 4–2 have become cult heroes and deservedly so because Sir Alf's team was the benchmark for success. Balanced throughout the side, England had strength, desire, world stars and a cutting edge.

Gordon Banks was excellent in goal throughout the 1966 tournament and, in my view, the best keeper England has produced. The thing about Banks was that he had great feet movement, but his save from Pele in the 1970 World Cup was not the normal Banks-type save because he did not have to dive very far. He got caught going in one direction, but switched the other way and stopped it going in the corner. Banks' quick feet got him into great positions. He possessed all the attributes of a class keeper in terms of shot stopping and commanding his penalty area.

Ray Wilson was arguably the best left back in the world at that particular time and really was a cultured, classy player. George Cohen was in at right back and maybe a tad fortunate to be the right man at the right time. George had replaced former England captain Jimmy Armfield and was, in many ways, a clone of Jimmy, which Alf obviously liked. George did not have the greatest ability in the world but was a solid defender and adept at overlapping. Jimmy was experienced, although knocking on a bit by 1966 and his best years were behind him, but was in the squad as back-up.

Jack Charlton, by his own admission, was not the best centre half about, but was the best combination for Bobby Moore. Big Jack was a moaner. 'Kick that chuffing ball away, get that chuffing ball out of the ground,' Jack would continually moan, but was the best foil for skipper Moore who was the only world class player who did not have searing pace off the mark. Bobby was sheer class and the coolest player in the side when it mattered. He was terrific in the final and set up two of the goals with pinpoint passes. With Big Jack screaming at him to kick the ball into Row Z, Bobby played in Hurst for his hat-trick goal.

The midfield required a player like Nobby Stiles to succeed and Nobby fitted the bill to perfection. Every team needs a player to break things up in front of the back four or man mark an opponent out of a game. This was Nobby's role and it allowed Bobby Charlton the freedom to play. When the press slated Nobby and called for him to be dropped during the tournament, following a challenge against a French opponent, Alf stuck by him. And Nobby came up trumps against Portugal and West Germany when England needed big performances. Nobby knew his role and did it to perfection. At that time, people didn't realise Nobby's pace. He was a flying machine over 10 to 15 yards, which is how he was able to stop Portuguese superstar Eusebio.

Bobby Charlton was a special player who had a thunderbolt shot in either foot. Not many people talk about it but Bobby also had pace and his other great asset was that he could distribute the ball, although it sometimes went astray. Alan Ball, God bless him, used to joke about this in his after-dinner speeches. Alan would jest, 'Bobby was great but he was not the poor bugger who had to chase around getting the misplaced passes. Bobby would drop the right shoulder, then left shoulder, hit the ball 50 yards before shrugging his shoulders and off I'd charge to retrieve to pass it back to him!'

As for Bally, he was the best player on the day when England lifted the World Cup. Bally was youngest, had most energy and had the cheek to run about telling elder statesman of the team what to do. And none of them could argue because they knew he was right. Bobby Charlton and Beckenbauer cancelled each other out and the German side went wrong in underestimating the impact that Bally could have. He had a storming game.

Pundits dubbed Martin Peters as being ahead of his time and there was no truer statement. Martin was a master of timing the late run at set pieces to score. A classy player, Martin ghosted into the box to strike with deadly accuracy. As for Roger Hunt, he was a far better player than pundits gave him credit for. Many unfairly cited him as a machine that got possession and scored goals. Roger was blessed with pace and great feet and was a clean striker of the ball. For me, there was little wonder he held so many Liverpool records for a long period.

As for Geoff Hurst, well, if ever there was a player who took his chance it was Geoff and it's hard to see his hat-trick in a final being repeated. Kempes, Rossi, Zidane and Ronaldo have all gone close in subsequent finals but none has matched Geoff on that sunny July afternoon. In the modern era, the game has changed so much that no team would leave themselves so wide open. With the advent of substitutes it's doubtful that it will happen because teams will shut up shop and not go for broke late on. In my lifetime, I cannot envisage a player notching a World Cup final hat-trick. Geoff, though, was a fine leader of the line, strong and with a clinical finish.

England won the World Cup because they had five world class players in the squad: Banks, Wilson, Moore, Charlton and Jimmy Greaves. Greaves was the one player who missed out on the great day, and what a talent he was. Denis Law was my all time hero but Greavsie was not far behind. My earliest memories of Jimmy go back to when he joined the legendary Tottenham double winning side of 1960–61. When Tottenham bought him for £99,999, they were all the rage the length and breadth of Britain. Greaves was a great footballer and, as I got to know him through the after-dinner circuit, I also discovered that he's a wonderful person.

Sitting down and talking with Jimmy was like chatting to my next door neighbour. Greavsie was always full of stories. During one conversation he got around to my old club Leeds United and facing the likes of Bremner, Giles and Hunter. Jimmy recalled competing against these lads in their pomp along with Big Jack, Clarke, Gray, Lorimer, Cooper and Jones. On the Thursday before an upcoming clash, Jimmy said to Bill Nicholson, 'I never get a kick at Elland Road so it's pointless taking me.'

Bill Nich said, 'Come on Greavsie you are going to go and play well, I don't want any negative talk. We are going to Elland Road and we'll win this time'.

At half time Tottenham were on the road to defeat and the players trudged into the away dressing room. Before Bill Nich could say anything Jimmy piped up, 'Boss, I did warn you!'

Jimmy had a terrific career, winning a couple of FA Cup winners medals but will always be remembered for the World Cup when he got a gash against France in the group stages and failed to get back into the starting line-up for the final against West Germany as Roger Hunt and Geoff Hurst took the striking roles. It is well documented that he never recovered from missing out, but if you talk to the entire England squad about recognised world players at Alf's disposal, to a man they cite Gordon Banks, Ray Wilson, Bobby Moore, Bobby Charlton and the magnificent scoring machine that was Jimmy Greaves.

Tragically for Jimmy, he did not figure in the final and pictures of the celebrating team show a stunned looking Jimmy congratulating his winning teammates. History demonstrates that Alf was right not to play him but indisputably at that level of football Greavsie was the greatest goal scorer the British game has produced. Never mind the likes of Dixie Dean (even though his goal-scoring feat of 60 league goals in a season will not be matched), Cloughie (in his all too short career of a goal a game for Middlesbrough in Division 2), Hurst, Law, Hunt and Clarke (in my era) and Rush, Lineker, Shearer, Owen and Rooney in more recent times. In my opinion, Jimmy Greaves was the greatest goal scorer this country has produced at the highest level of the game. Jimmy struck 44 goals in 49 games for England, a stunning ratio, when the standard was far harder to strike.

Whenever you talk about great players you talk about pace and Jimmy had phenomenal pace. The year I joined Forest, Greavsie scored two cracking goals in the FA Cup semi-final at Hillsborough to send all Forest supporters home devastated. His speed and reactions were amazing. Jimmy possessed terrific sure footedness and I recall him scoring a goal for Tottenham at Nottingham Forest. I was watching by the tunnel in the pen where young apprentices stood. Tottenham took a corner and

Jimmy was by the six-yard box on the far side of the goal from the corner. It landed knee high to Jimmy when he side-footed it home into the net for a great strike. I was standing next to Alan Buckley who turned to me and said, 'I'm sure he meant that.'

I said, 'I'm chuffing sure he meant it.' It was some finish and I could only marvel at his talent. Greavsie was some player.

England heroes of the sixties aside, it was now my turn to impress and I tried my damndest but it was not to be. The biggest disappointment of my career was not representing England but it was not for want of trying during the many international camps that I attended. While I failed to gain a full cap, other Fancy Dans did make the grade, but in the main only for a short run of games. Rodney Marsh won nine caps, Frank Worthington claimed eight, Stan Bowles made five appearances and Alan Hudson got the nod twice. This quartet was made up of superb ball players who should all have won a hatful of caps. In the end they did win the ultimate accolade, which was something that passed me by.

Sadly I played in an era when a ball player was frowned upon in many quarters. Tony Currie was a classic example. A star at Sheffield United when he made his full international debut for England, Tony was a classy attacking midfield player of his generation at the highest level. His main attribute was an ability to pass over any distance with pinpoint accuracy, but he also had a devastating shot. Tony played in an infamous World Cup qualifying encounter against Poland in October 1973 at Wembley. The match ended in a 1–1 draw, knocking England out of the finals in Germany. Many believe the 1974 squad with the backbone of the side made up of Shilton, Madeley, Hughes, Bell, Hunter, Ball, Currie, Clarke and Channon had a terrific chance of success but it was not to be.

Norman is a pal and a great lad but against Poland he broke his own cardinal rule of playing safety first and taking no chances. Instead of kicking the ball into Row Z, Norman attempted to keep the ball in play and launch an attack as England struggled to break down a stubborn Poland side. England lost possession and Poland broke swiftly to score. England failed to qualify and Sir Alf Ramsey ultimately got the sack. So who did England drop after a subsequent friendly defeat to Italy? They dropped the one truly ball-playing player who could turn a game in the side, Currie, who was a prodigious talent. At the time I thought this was bizarre. Tony would not play for England over the coming two seasons and did not regain a regular place until the 1977–78 campaign when he took his tally to 17 caps, a ludicrous amount for his talent.

Arguably the most fearsome tackler of my generation, 'Bites Yer Legs' Hunter was chalk and cheese when it came to his personality on and off the field. On the pitch, Norman was tough as old boots and could crunch players in tackles. Never dirty, the odd challenge was a shade late but there was never any intent. Off the field, though, Norman was the opposite in terms of temperament and the first to praise skill, including my own ability. Norman used to say he'd give his right arm for half my ability, which was a tremendous accolade as he was some player. But pundits did not always share Norman's sentiment. Neither did managers who felt the more ability players had the less inclined they were to graft. That type of criticism was directed at so-called English mavericks, ball players like Bowles, Marsh, Worthington, not to forget George Best who graced the Northern Ireland team.

None of these lads ran around like blue-arsed flies all over a pitch and they did not always get stuck into the muck and nettle stuff but they could turn a game with a moment of magic. When

TV programmes look back at the greats from the sixties and seventies they always show iconic moments of Bestie and co. And so they should, but football is not just about the goal scorers and dribblers. It's also about uncompromising defenders such as Hunter and his like. There is little footage shown of a hard, tough defender making tackles and scrapping away for the cause of his team. On the other hand, footage is always resurrected of Bestie, God rest his soul, being harassed by Chelsea hard man 'Chopper' Harris and his best efforts to scythe him down. It's a classic piece of action as Bestie evades lunge after lunge. The defensive tactics of Hunter and Harris would not last five minutes in the modern game, but it does demonstrate what strikers had to put up with in terms of challenges from behind.

Despite not making the full England side, travelling with the squad gave me a terrific insight to my fellow entertainers. Stan Bowles plied his trade at Queens Park Rangers, was a wonderful talent but one on his own. Before a Home International match against Northern Ireland I stayed overnight at his flat in Shepherd's Bush. Next morning I got up but there was no sight of Stan. I hung around and realised I'd be late. Joe Mercer was caretaker-manager. I rang him to explain the situation but Joe Cool was relaxed. 'Don't worry son,' he said, 'I've had this before with Stan, get yourself in a taxi you won't be in trouble for being late.' At the team hotel, Stan rolled up with a wry smile.

A week earlier England had defeated Wales 2–0 at Ninian Park. I sat on the bench waiting for my opportunity and wearing my spare set of boots with moulded studs. Stan scored the opening goal wearing my first choice boots, as the day before he'd sold his boots to make a bet! Stan said, 'You'd better hope I come off, Duncan.' I was not happy. Sitting on the bench was something I'd get used to. I was there again when Stan played in a win over Northern Ireland and Keith Weller, who made his debut against Wales, scored. No disrespect to Keith, God bless him, but I failed to understand why he got the nod ahead of me. There was no question in my mind that I offered a bigger threat as an attacking force.

Further disappointment followed a 2–2 draw with Argentina at Wembley when I joined a post-season England trip to Eastern Europe playing matches in East Germany, Bulgaria and Yugoslavia. Joe Mercer's squad was arguably the most flamboyant squad for some time. All the so-called Fancy Dans were present and I was all but told that I'd get a game, which I took at face value. In Leipzig—the greyest, most miserable place ever—the moment we left the hotel, guys in full leather coats and trilby hats followed us everywhere. We had no idea if the guards were for protection or not but their presence was unnerving. Despite the security restrictions, touring with the England boys was terrific even if I was official skip carrier and joker. After a 1–1 draw against East Germany and a 1–0 win over Bulgaria we travelled to Belgrade to face Yugoslavia.

I'd pulled on the famous white shirt and sat on the bench thinking that surely this was going to be my chance. We trained at the Army ground, a massive stadium where the match was scheduled to take place. Before the game, Billy Wright came over to me and said, 'Congratulations son, all the best.'

I thought, 'Here we go again, am I the last to know? Am I playing or not?'

As it turned out I was on the bench again but felt I'd be coming on for my first cap at some stage. In the dressing room even the lads felt sorry for me as I was the only one in the squad not to have played a game. Kevin Keegan turned to me before the game and said, 'Dunc, if we get in front I'll go down 10 minutes from time and you'll get on.'

I thought, 'You'll do for me pal.'

Ten minutes from time with the score at 2–2, Joe put on Malcolm Macdonald for Frank Worthington and he missed a sitter with his first kick. Kevin looked over and shrugged his shoulders. I was speechless and thought, 'Thanks SuperMac.'

Playing away from home brought bizarre incidents and at times hostile crowds, especially for an England-Scotland clash at Hampden Park. Although both sets of players respected each other, there was no love lost on the park. This was even more apparent with the reaction of the Tartan Army. Driving towards Hampden we ended up surrounded by a group determined to welcome us in true Scottish spirit. The lads exchanged a few anxious looks as a not-so friendly bunch rocked our coach. I was on the bench for the game and the intimidating atmosphere did not stop throughout the match. There was plenty of verbal from a partisan crowd and the odd bottle and missile raining towards us, but it was all good natured!

After several years of close calls, my final opportunity for a full cap came after Bob Latchford gained selection for England following Everton's great start to the 1977–78 campaign. Steve Burtenshaw wanted Ron Greenwood, who had replaced Don Revie as manager, to play Bob alongside Dave Thomas and myself. We worked well as a unit at Everton and Steve felt we could do the same for England. Steve made the point to Ron that Everton had the only all-English forward line and we knew each other's game inside out. Dave got crosses in, Bob finished them off but I took pressure off both players. Steve told Ron that whatever he thought of me with my tricks and flicks, I was a box-to-box player. One minute I'd be near our penalty box, next thing I'd win a corner but people didn't notice that when they were having a knock at me. Steve also noted that while Dave would provide a cross for Bob to tuck the ball away, when pundits analysed where the goal came from, they'd not always recall it started with me. As it transpired I didn't get a call up but having Steve on my side was welcome news.

Making the England squad and failing to gain a full cap was hard to take but being selected was out of my hands. At the time there were dozens of players vying for striking roles in the side including Macdonald, Worthington, Keegan, Channon and Clarke. I could say flippantly that if I was a better player then I'd have played but it's not so straightforward. I do take solace that there was so much strength in depth in terms of attackers. I was part of the scene, trained with the elite of English football and got close but it was not be.

Life is strange, however, because after hanging up my boots I did finally receive an invitation to represent my country, albeit in a veteran's World Cup tournament for the past six winners of the trophy in 1989. I jumped at the opportunity. England took part in the Copa Pele in Brazil and I was the only member of the England squad who had not been capped but I was not complaining, as it was a wonderful experience. In the squad, I lined up alongside former internationals Ray Clemence, Bobby Moore, Martin Peters, Norman Hunter and Peter Osgood. And we had a tough task on our hands because among the many stars participating were Brazil giants Rivelino, Socrates and Zico, Italian legends Paulo Rossi and Franco Causio, Argentine heroes Mario Kempes and Ricky Villa, while Franz Beckenbauer, Uwe Seeler and Wolfgang Overath lined up for Germany. Uruguay were the weakest side but did have Oscar Más in the team. The players took the round-robin tournament semi-seriously and in the end, not too surprisingly, Brazil were crowned champions.

In terms of modern day England there are nowhere near as many strikers to choose from and a problematic aspect is that the national team has suffered as a result of the foreign influx of players. The Premier League has the largest percentage of foreign players based in England. It's well documented and it is a growing problem. Now you could be cynical and say there has only ever been one great international team and that was in 1966 when Sir Alf, Bobby Moore and co ruled the world because we won. In 1970, many, like me, thought we had a better team than in 1966 but then the older generation talk about the Tom Finney and Stanley Matthews era prior to that. The fact remains that the England team has not performed, apart from in 1966, and we seem to be surprised at global tournaments when successive teams fail to deliver.

Currently we have had a golden era of players such as Beckham, Owen, Gerrard, Ferdinand, Terry and Rooney but even they have got nowhere near the likes of Lineker and Shearer when they led the line in teams that reached the semi-finals of the World Cup in 1990 and Euro Championships in 1996. The bottom line is that none of the big clubs really want their top stars to play international football in case they get injured. That is the reality of the situation so the manager has a constant problem of balancing technically less-gifted players with qualifying for tournaments and then having a squad that plays far more games than its European counterparts.

It may sound obvious when I say that you only need a balanced squad with a magical 11 but it's not so simple. This is because there are no youngsters learning from top players, as they cannot force their way into the top sides that are packed with top foreign stars. This catch-22 situation will not alter unless radical changes are made at the top of the Football Association but with freedom of contract it is impossible. Sadly, the reality is that we have to stop expecting to have a great England team. There are too many problems and the clubs are too powerful.

Nevertheless, Fabio Capello has got off to a terrific start and although he has a great track record, his appointment as England manager was, in my view, surprising. The obvious choice was Harry Redknapp who would have received universal support from players and supporters. I know he is settled at Tottenham Hotspur but Harry would have got my vote. Capello has impressed but his appointment is a step in the wrong direction. If we win the World Cup then the FA will be vindicated but it still sends the wrong signal to young English managers.

In my era, the situation was straightforward because foreign managers did not come into the equation. There was never any chance that Bill Shankly would have been offered, or taken, the top job when Sir Alf was sacked. You could read the script when Don Revie got the nod. But the Football Association was left with a bloody nose with Revie, so instead of picking the obvious choice in terms of Brian Clough, they took a safe pair of hands when they chose Ron Greenwood. Ron is a lovely man but he was not going to deliver the World Cup. Cloughie was off the wall and the best person to deliver the goods. The Football Association should have looked at the bigger picture because we suffered for years.

Not winning global honours, sadly, is all too realistic but I hope I'm proved wrong because I'd love to see England win the World Cup again in my lifetime as it was such a wonderful experience to be part of as a teenager in 1966. The atmosphere at home was amazing and gave the whole country a lift. Just look at the reaction to the England rugby union team when they won the World Cup in 2003, the England Ashes team in 2005 and GB Olympic winners from Beijing. The difference in all these sports was that the national team came before club sides. Fitness came first so international displays were not compromised. I for one, though, will be cheering from my settee if we pull it off under Capello with Ferdinand, Gerrard, Rooney and all the current lads in South Africa, 2010.

11

LIFE ON CIVVY STREET

Football had been my professional life for 15 years, but adjusting to the real world was not too onerous. Dot ran flower shops. One was in Anfield, which we sold to buy another in Newton-in-the-Willows. One day Dot informed me that she'd bought me a fruit 'n' veg shop in Prescott. I thought, 'Thank you very much!' Well, there was only one thing to do. I bought a van and for a few years joined the real world. It was a fantastic little business. I did the buying and selling but unfortunately the main employer in the area, BICC, cut its workforce drastically so there was little trade. The town effectively died for my business. When rates and rent increased, I returned the keys and moved on to a new life. I've been fortunate throughout my life because as one door shuts another one seems to open. And before long, I was working as a match summariser on local radio, opinionated hack, after-dinner speaker and television football pundit. The variety of work seemed a natural mix for my commitments.

There was never any chance that I'd stay in the game full time on the coaching or managerial side. Many lads hoped to stop in the game but it was not for me. After being involved with people like Cloughie and Shanks, I saw how tough the job can be. Football management was only for a certain type of individual. In recent years I've done a spot of coaching with kids at summer camps organised by my former Leeds colleague Paul Reaney, which has been great fun. I take skill sessions and, even though I can't run the way I once could, the old magic is still there when it comes to juggling a football. Such skills never leave you. My old chums Norman Hunter and Allan Clarke are also around so it's tremendous fun. I enjoy seeing my former team mates at either Leeds United or Everton when I do corporate hospitality engagements. And meeting great characters in the game has aided me with plenty of tales for the after-dinner circuit. Reminiscing about my career is second nature.

My first dalliance with radio came about prior to my Everton days and I was lucky enough to start with the very best, the late great Peter Jones in 1976. I was a match summariser at the FA Cup final when Southampton defeated Manchester United and then when England faced Scotland in the Home International championships. I enjoyed both occasions immensely and welcomed other opportunities when they came up.

Shortly after I had signed for Everton, Radio City in Liverpool was looking for two footballers to head up a new-style football show called *Mac 'n' Tosh*. They selected Liverpool striker John Toshack, who was popular with Reds supporters, and me as Everton's latest big money signing. I have to admit that I was amazed to receive the invitation but it sounded a terrific opportunity and I've always been one for new challenges. We interviewed current stars and former heroes on top of offering a forum for fans to discuss topical stories.

Current players hosting a chat show on radio was a new phenomenon in 1977 and I was delighted to help blaze a trail. *Mac 'n' Tosh* quickly adopted a cult status. We started green as grass but had wonderful talent behind the scenes in Richard Keys, Clive Tyldesley, Elton Welsby and Paul Davis. All moved on to terrific success. To add a local feel, local broadcasters in the Merseyside area were part of the team. There was lots of input on programming material and Polydor treated us like DJs by sending big hits of the day to play.

The format of the show was fast and furious to keep listeners interested. It was tremendous fun and I had to become something of a mimic on occasions as some guests failed to turn up. John and I interviewed all the leading characters in football, past and present, and we had a section where fans phoned in. We interviewed everyone locally from Bill Shankly to Bob Paisley for the latest gossip. And through interviewing Don Revie, Brian Clough and Malcolm Allison, we got the lowdown from a managerial perspective internationally and domestically. Naturally we quizzed star players like Kevin Keegan, Liam Brady, Andy Gray, Charlie George, Mick Mills, Peter Lorimer, Frank Worthington, Pat Jennings, Colin Bell, Lou Macari, Malcolm Macdonald, Gerry Francis, Steve Perryman, Trevor Brooking, Archie Gemmell and Steve Coppell. Away from the stars of the game we also chatted to football commentators such as Brian Moore and Peter Jones, football fans like model Twiggy and Justin Hayward of Moody Blues fame, and many football-mad comedians such as Jimmy Tarbuck.

Everyone had tales to share. Tarby was full of gags throughout the interview, while meeting Twiggy was potluck. Her father played for Preston North End and she happened to be at a game I was at, so the interview worked well. Chatting to Twiggy was not difficult but she could not stop laughing throughout so it took longer than planned. The editing lads had to work overtime on subbing it down. On another occasion when Liverpool played Norwich City, Tosh interviewed Norwich boss John Bond after the match. In a frank question, Tosh asked why John never seemed to discuss particular issues at Norwich, yet was happy to chat about other clubs' shortfalls. It was a leading question and the Norwich manager said it was one of the best questions he'd been asked, but, expert that he was, still managed to dodge answering it.

Chat show programmes were not as widespread as the phone-ins that have sprung up locally and nationally in recent years. We just had a 10-minute slot on the show. The programme lasted two years until John joined Swansea as player-manager. Radio City wanted Ray Clemence to take over from John but I was uncomfortable building a new media partnership, as the crack would not be the same. Mick Lyons teamed up with Ray but the show fizzled out.

I'm not sure why Radio City chose me but they must have thought I was a reasonable interviewee at Everton and in fairness to them, I was always willing to give pre- and post-match interviews. Luckily for me, I was in the right place at the right time and it formed a bridge to a new career. Media partnerships need a spark of magic and Tosh was the perfect foil to my style of broadcasting, which was in your face at 90 miles an hour. Tosh had a dry sense of humour and was impossible if Liverpool lost, which was a rare occasion. Having learned my trade at Nottingham Forest, I knew how to lose before winning so accepted defeat far more graciously. Tosh and I became great mates, and our friendship has lasted down the years.

We recorded the programme on a Sunday morning and it aired at 5.05–6 p.m. Each week we knew whom we'd be seeing at a game or if we were not in action, we went to a midweek game instead. I'd always take a recording machine and grab someone for an interview. The experience held me in good stead for the after-dinner circuit in years to come as it armed me with a plethora of anecdotes. Talking at length is second nature to me, and mimicking the likes of Cloughie has been a real asset. *Mac* 'n' *Tosh* was a great, innovative venture at the time. A lot of local football headlines on a Monday came from our show because guests did not talk to us as they would journalists. We chatted like mates. It made fascinating listening and station audience figures quickly grew.

Although I'd done the occasional spot of summarising at matches, it really picked up after I'd hung up my boots. This particular avenue started with Radio Merseyside when football was not as huge as it is today. It was easier to get a foothold and I was the equivalent of current aficionados Mark Lawrenson and Jimmy Armfield. And I really enjoyed it. Of course, working for local radio you cannot help but be a shade biased—okay really biased—but you have to criticise when it's relevant and I've never been afraid to do this.

Shortly after the match summarising road started, I received a call from the BBC asking me to host a radio phone-in show called 606 after Danny Baker had hosted the programme. The opportunity came my way after I did a one off guest appearance with ex-Chelsea legend Peter Osgood. Incredibly the BBC was going to scrap the schedule as they thought phone-in shows might have run their course, an unbelievable thought today. I hosted four shows from a Manchester studio but producers wanted a host in London so I agreed to troop down south once a week. Of course, now it does not matter where you transmit from but that was the nature of the beast at the time. It was a great experience and I enjoyed many infamous moments.

The show was live, as it is today, and on one show when I asked what problems Barnet FC were experiencing, club chairman Stan Flashman rang up and let slip he'd paid players in readies. Phone lines were red hot and we ended up on *News at Ten*! Stan allegedly had to answer a few awkward questions over the coming days. And then there was Benny the Halifax Town cat, which was a concocted story taken out of context. During the show a call came up on my monitor that producers were desperate for me to take. 'Duncan, Big John here.'

I said, 'It's John McGrath, manager of Halifax Town, previously centre half with Newcastle United and Southampton.' I welcomed the big fellow on to the show and asked what he wanted to share with the nation. John said he'd been listening and heard there were 10,000 fans locked out of Newcastle United's St James' Park ground. John wanted to bus them all to Halifax to cheer on his lads. Of course, it was all a bit of a giggle. I asked how things were going at The Shay in Halifax. John said things were so hard they could not afford to feed Benny the cat. I hoped there would be a reaction but was not prepared for what occurred as the BBC and Halifax were inundated with cat food, postal orders and cheques for Benny. The story was picked up by the television boys and a reporter was sent to Halifax to record a piece with Big John. He told club chairman George Mulhall that the BBC was coming to do a piece with Benny and him. George was dumbfounded and told John to find a cat sharpish, adding, 'Make sure it's a thin'un!' I enjoyed working on the show, however fleetingly. They were real pioneering days for football talk shows.

Penning an opinionated column for the *Today* newspaper, based in London, came out of the blue in the late eighties and the column ran until the early nineties. Dave Alexander, an old hack, helped me enormously and I was extremely grateful for his expertise because I had no formal training. I got on with journalists at all the clubs I played for and was always happy to give a quote before or after a game. A lot of the lads were sceptical about giving interviews on the basis that they may be misquoted but I never understood that attitude. Nowadays it is impossible for hacks as sadly a press officer is always in tow chaperoning stars of today. The media, in the main, during my era were pussycats and journalists in general never misinterpreted my comments. In any case I have always believed that all publicity, if you were in control, was good publicity.

As with my introduction to radio and after-dinner speaking, once again, I appeared to be in the right place at the right time. I was initially offered the opportunity to write one article and the first time I phoned down my copy, to my relief, sub-editors stuck it in word for word. I wasn't promoting myself but editors were happy to let my new fledgling writing career develop. Articles I wrote related to issues of the day and concentrated on surprise, surprise, Manchester United (wherever possible), Liverpool, Arsenal and Tottenham Hotspur. Characters providing a nationwide interest at the time included Alex Ferguson, Brian Clough, Bryan Robson, Kenny Dalglish, George Graham and Paul Gascoigne. Punters didn't really want in-depth comments on smaller clubs, it had to be the big boys and even though United, managed at the time by Big Ron Atkinson, were not winning titles every year they were still big news. And Big Ron was always good for a story. I was told to make my articles snappy, topical and contentious otherwise nobody read them. It was unnerving but also provided a tremendous adrenaline rush.

My association with after-dinner speaking at corporate and sporting events started in 1977 while I was an Everton player. It all began when Tranmere Rovers chairman, Bill Bothwell, rang to tell me they had been let down by a speaker and wondered if I'd help bail the club out. Tranmere were a forward thinking club. They switched home games to a Friday night to attract more spectators as they were in competition with Liverpool and Everton, and were also one of the first football clubs in the country to hold regular business dinners. Bill was a persuasive character and before I knew it, I had agreed to step in.

Bill was confident in my ability to deliver an interesting, informative, anecdotal and witty address even though I'd not spoken publically before, apart from telling the odd tale to the lads on coach journeys to while away the hours when we were not playing cards. Bill had heard me present *Mac 'n' Tosh* and felt sure I'd be a smash hit. Of course, I realised where Bill was coming from in his persuasive arguments for me to take part. I was an Everton player, popular with Evertonians, had a weekly spot on local radio, was recognised as a bit of a character and could spin a few tales. Bill said, 'Look Duncan don't worry about it, just stand up and tell a few stories and the punters will love it.' Before I knew it, a packed house was laughing along to my football-related stories. The evening, I had to admit, was a blast and I really enjoyed it. Bill was right and quick to tell me so. I should never have doubted Bill in the first place because he knew his audience and started me, unknowingly, down a path that I am still thankfully treading today.

As luck would have it Murray Birnie was among the guests in the audience and happened to be fundraising director at Bury FC. Murray was also involved at Lancashire CCC, organising stalwart cricketer Jack Simmons' testimonial dinner, so it was not long before I was telling some more gags about my days at Nottingham Forest when I idolised Notts cricketing legend Sir Garfield Sobers. I also added a few anecdotes about my old mate Derek 'Rags' Randall. Again the presentation was a hit and I soon repeated the exercise with a few more cricketing laughs at a testimonial bash for Lancashire and West Indies legendary skipper Clive Lloyd.

A new career was dawning but I had to limit the invites, as I was still a professional footballer. I enjoyed it, the punters liked my style, but as my football career was in full throttle, I only spoke at the occasional event. Once retired, though, I was delighted to hop back into the industry, which was still in its infancy during the early eighties. At an early Rotary dinner, I was guest speaker along with a comedian called Stan Mortensen. I thought, 'It can't be the same Stan Mortensen who scored a hat-trick in the famous 1953 Matthews final?' I was gobsmacked because it turned out to be the former Blackpool and England centre-forward. Morty was a goal scoring machine, notching nearly 200 goals for the Seasiders on top of hitting 23 goals in 25 England appearances, this was some scoring ratio.

Stan, by this time, was a milliner and did a spot of stand-up comedy. We had a brief chat and then Stan was on. He stood up and his opening gag knocked me for six! 'Gentlemen,' Stan said, 'Good evening, you might wonder why a person who has scored a hat-trick in an FA Cup final is billed as a comedian. Well, when you have scored a hat-trick in an FA Cup final and it's named after somebody else, referring to Sir Stanley Matthews, you can stick the game of football as far up your arses as you can get it.' Stan got a laugh but came across as somewhat bitter, yet who could blame him? Nobody had matched his feat for 30 years and we are still waiting for another FA Cup final hat-trick over half a century later. Stan Matthews, to his defence, has always stated that the triumph should have been known as Morty's final but the press boys dubbed it the 'Matthews' final and it's stuck ever since.

I never went close to achieving what Stan did that memorable day but if I had notched a hat-trick, I'd have made sure it was not just known as the Matthews final. Stan Matthews was an iconic figure and made the winning goal, which was a significant contribution, but Morty should have grabbed the national headlines. I got to know Morty on the circuit and he was a lovely man. The day he died in 1991, Blackpool played at Wembley against Torquay United in a Fourth Division playoff final. A minute's silence was held before the game and his former club has honoured his memory since with a statue in front of Bloomfield Road's North Stand.

Over the years, I became more in demand and it has been a fast, furious lifestyle. Of course, constant engagements build up my profile and when the Premier League kicked off, I was well positioned as the after-dinner circuit took on a new lease of life. Apart from business luncheons, hospitality organisers at football clubs wanted ex-players on a match day for corporate entertainment and it's still going strong, which is terrific. Being involved at both Everton and Leeds United is always enjoyable from both the punters' and ex-players' perspective.

Everything seemed to happen together with radio and after-dinner speaking opportunities and it was not long before openings as a football pundit came up first on local television and then on national and digital channels with Sky Sports. Local TV was a great way to get involved in this media format because I knew what to expect when national producers approached me. Historically, there were two pre-match television shows on a Saturday, which were prime time before games kicked off at 3 p.m. BBC's *Football Focus* had seen a number of presenters over the years become household names including Sam Leach, Frank Bough, Des Lynam and Bob Wilson. ITV had a rival pre-match football programme called *On The Ball* presented by Brian Moore, who was an institution when it came to football presenting, so I was taken aback when I was first approached to take over the slot with a new updated show.

To the surprise of everyone I knew in the media world, I declined the offer as it was not the right time. ITV replaced the show with *Saint and Greavsie* hosted by sixties legends Ian St John and Jimmy Greaves. The programme developed a cult following and it was wonderful seeing Saint develop from appearing wooden to a consummate presenter while Greavsie was a natural from day one. Nothing fazed Jimmy and I loved seeing the goal scoring great in action. Greavsie never appeared to take himself, or the programme, too seriously, even though he was deadly serious about it, and as a result was the perfect foil for Saint. As a double act they are arguably the best partnership there has been in this format of football shows.

Sky Sports coverage has of course changed the landscape for the watching public but I am pleased to see that *Match of the Day* has survived as a footballing institution. Gary Lineker has developed his own style to become the undisputed number one anchor man after hanging up his boots, while a number of pundits have carved out a niche following successful playing days from the football fraternity. The likes of Andy Gray, Alan Hansen, Ally McCoist, Mark Lawrenson and Andy Townsend have all gone on to become household names again.

Over the years, I've been involved with football punditry on television from time to time. Hosting Everton TV when it initially came out on satellite television was groundbreaking at the time and all clubs have that facility nowadays. My involvement with football on television centred initially on Sky Sports screening the *Footballers Football Show*. Ex-players discussed the game and suddenly a whole new arena opened up for former footballers who had the ability to chat. Naturally a number of ex-pros tried to jump on the bandwagon but soon got caught out as it was not just a matter of turning up and talking. You had to be able to be articulate and opinionated in a discussion. Many players far more famous than me came along and soon disappeared but for the likes of George Best, Rodney Marsh and Jimmy Greaves there were plenty of openings with TV, newspapers and after-dinner speaking.

When I signed my first professional contract at Nottingham

Forest, Bestie was the one footballer pulling in the crowds, pundits and plaudits from around the world. Though George never played in a global tournament, he was European Footballer of the Year at his peak and rightly so. Our careers never crossed as players but I was delighted to work with him on the after-dinner circuit. I was also privileged to see him at close quarters, but turned down the opportunity to tour Britain as part of the *George Best Show* prior to the Best/Marsh forums. I thanked George at the time as I felt that doing so many events would have limited future opportunities. Fans wanted to hear George Best every day of the week but I was no George Best. On the circuit, I am delighted to be a name but George was quite literally in a league of his own.

Bestie was the first football megastar. Denis Law always maintains that George was everybody's blue-eyed boy, but in particular he was a favourite of Matt Busby. Bestie got away with a lot of things that other players with far less ability got caught out on, because of his talent. George never saw anything he did as being a problem to himself or anyone else until it was too late. George was an intelligent guy, knew exactly what he was and the impact he had, but didn't know how to handle the fame. He did everything to excess and he was the first football superstar in the modern era of the swinging sixties in the days before agents controlled every aspect of dealings including image rights. People talk about the hype behind David Beckham, but that is nothing compared to the hype behind George Best, especially when you consider that back then there was no Internet or global media circus.

I was once on a flight for a few hours with George and chatted to him throughout the journey. He readily admitted that he never knew what George Best was going to do tomorrow let alone what George Best did yesterday. Bestie was a victim of not being carefully managed at his peak. George, at times, was his own worst enemy but as Denis Law once told me, and it's well documented, Matt Busby had to take some of the blame for being too lenient with him. Matt looked upon George as a son but it's difficult to criticise those closest to him because Bestie was unique in terms of his status. However, the hangers on looking for a fast buck did George no favours when you look back at his life.

I'd hazard a guess that more words have been spoken and written about George than any other footballer to play the beautiful game with, arguably, only Pele edging him. For all his failings surrounding drink, and they have been well documented, as George said before his death, supporters will remember him for his football when everything else is long forgotten. That was Bestie—everyone has a favourite memory about him. There were many great days for Manchester United domestically and in Europe but my top reminiscence was when he represented his country. It is still lodged clearly in my memory and I relate it whenever I get the opportunity to pay tribute to the great man. The match concerned was when George played for Northern Ireland against Scotland. The result was George Best 1 Scotland 0. That game has gone down in folklore for the people of Northern Ireland. Bestie's memory always brings a feeling of sadness that he has gone, but joy as to what he left behind. Whenever I travel to Belfast for a corporate event and arrive at the George Best Airport it's a surreal feeling. I'm just so privileged to have known him even for a fleeting time.

Pundits, together with football followers, love to debate and talk about legends of the game and who can blame them because star players are what make the game. For me, apart from Bestie, only Pele and arguably Maradona match up in terms of true global recognition. From the mid-sixties to early seventies

Eusebio, Moore, Bobby Charlton, Beckenbauer, Muller, Rivelino, Gerson, Tostao, Jairzinho and Cryuff and since the likes of Socrates, Zico, Ronaldo, Zidane, Beckham and Kaka have deservedly been recognised as world class but are they at the same level as Best, Pele and Maradona? In my opinion, they are not quite as good, but some might disagree.

Pele, for me, was the greatest player of his generation. I saw footage of Pele at the Word Cup in 1958, 1962 and 1970, and I could only marvel because he was simply awesome. Pele had strength, remarkable power in his shooting, terrific technique and, above all, an aura about him that still exists today. As for Maradona, he also had a special quality that marked him out. Some of his goals at the 1986 World Cup for Argentina, bar the 'Hand of God' goal, were superlative but more than that, Maradona carried the team. England fans will always feel cheated by his first effort in a quarter-final clash but Maradona's second was out of this world by anyone's standards and he was the star performer of the tournament. Pele is an ambassador for the game and travels the world while Maradona has overcome a bad-boy reputation to take the helm of the Argentine national side. It will be interesting to see how he fares at the World Cup in South Africa. On the pitch, Maradona's side will be scrutinised while off it, Maradona will receive more media attention than his players. It promises to be a fascinating ride.

I was fortunate to play against most of the greats from the 1966 World Cup side and world class players at Manchester United, Leeds United, Liverpool, Arsenal, Everton, West Ham, Manchester City and Tottenham Hotspur. When I played against Bobby Moore, he had something that made him stand out as a footballer. Bobby looked a bit on the chubby side, was not particularly great in the air or particularly quick, so why was he such a great and well respected player around the world? Sport is all about timing. Bobby made plenty of time to play the ball and to make a decision on when to tackle or pass. Jimmy Greaves was a striker who caressed the football and his initial touch was first rate. It was also no coincidence that Bobby and Jimmy alongside key players such as Denis Law, Colin Bell, Billy Bremner, Alan Ball and Martin Peters from top teams, made the right decision at a critical moment. All these players found a yard of space but when they got the ball, their decision-making was generally the right one. And the further up the pitch you went, the more players like Bestie, Leeds' Eddie Gray and Celtic giant Jimmy 'Jinky' Johnstone had a licence to be expressive.

Wilf McGuinness was briefly the Manchester United boss and he told a lovely tale about George on the after-dinner circuit. The incident remains crystal clear as Wilf recalled George flying down the wing with the ball at his feet. As George waltzed past the opposing full back, Denis Law made a great run into the penalty area. Wilf screamed to George to give the ball to Denis but George cut back inside and beat another opponent. Denis made a second run and Wilf screamed again, 'Give the ball to Denis!' but George carried on the run as Denis looked for another opening. Wilf was going crazy in the dugout and screamed for a third time, 'Give the ball to . . . Oh great goal George!' Wilf acknowledged in his tale that as a full back he could not comprehend what Bestie had in mind as he was quite simply a genius on the football field.

Of the many stars that I didn't face, I'd like to have been on the same pitch, albeit from the opposing end, as Portuguese legend Eusebio, who had incredible strength, pace and a fearsome shot. And then there were the likes of Di Stefano and Puskas who starred for Real Madrid over many years and instigated the annihilation of Eintracht Frankfurt in an unforgettable European Cup final at Hampden Park. Di Stefano scored four and Puskas grabbed a hat-trick during a 7–3 classic. Real's display was seen as the best attacking performance ever. And then there are the clips of Stanley Matthews with his hands on his hips waiting on the halfway line for the ball before going on a run, and the clips of Tom Finney who appeared to have incredible pace. The 100 metres world record has come down by a few tenths since the fifties, so on a football pitch the actual physical ability of a player has always been there. Modern techniques have brought out more of an athlete. Today there are wonderful players such as Gerrard, Torres, Rooney and Ronaldo but the likes of Shackleton, Mortensen, Lofthouse, Charles and Lawton were similar in days gone by. And then there were great keepers such as Yashin of USSR and Gilmar of Brazil. Players who faced these keepers say they were awesome. As the game has evolved you have to admire all these individuals because they are the stars who inspired the next generation to play the game. All these players were exceptional talents, but for me Pele, Best and Maradona transcend all others.

Of course, the World Cup Boys of 1966 have proved a smash hit on the after-dinner scene. Nobby Stiles, Jack Charlton, Alan Ball, Bobby Charlton, Geoff Hurst, Martin Peters and Gordon Banks have enjoyed plenty of work, and all have different styles. Football fans love hearing tales from England's greatest sporting achievement. I've been at many a do when the lads have spoken. To single just three of the lads out, Big Jack, Nobby and Bally (God bless him), always played a blinder every time they spoke, with guests lapping up every story. Big Jack never fails to impress when he reminisces about Sir Alf in his posh voice, while Nobby always brings the house down when he recalls his man-to-man escapades and Ballie in his high-pitched voice delivered cracks with ease.

Away from the Boys of 1966, punters wanted more variety of

stars so Ryder Cup lads, Rugby Union Grand Slam and World Cup heroes, together with cricketing legends, have all done well. While I have been fortunate, and privileged, to move up the so-called speakers' ladder as the circuit has evolved from the sixties and seventies lads, so characters like Matthew Le Tissier and Paul Merson have made a massive impression in recent years. Looking back to when it all started at Tranmere three decades ago, if anyone had said to me I'd speak at Windsor Castle and on cruise liners I'd have said they were mad. It's been a phenomenal ride and long may it continue.

Since the Premier League era began at the onset of the 1992–93 season it has been really busy on the circuit with plenty of ex-pros joining the ranks of after-dinner speakers. But in some ways the golden years have gone because at one time there were only around half a dozen ex-players who spoke regularly. This was because not everyone was capable of doing it. Many lads tried but would have been better advised to stay away as they were not competent in putting an address together. The whole exercise proved embarrassing for them. They traded off their name but it's not as simple as that. All stories are based around the truth but punters know there is always a bit of poetic licence, which makes the tales what they are, pure nostalgia. I was a sub for England against Scotland once and I mention that Denis Law was present. Denis had actually retired then but it's great to talk about my all-time hero. Punters would always rather hear a story about Denis than a player no one remembers with such affection.

An area that is slightly easier for ex-players is Question and Answer Sessions but you still have to be articulate. Sitting on a panel or splitting an address with a Question and Answer Session is always great fun as you never know what questions will come up. In the main, questions revolve around numerous topics including legends, great games, hooliganism, the Big Four, Champions League, spiralling salaries, impact of agents, whether the game is heading for financial meltdown, technology and everyone's favourite, the much maligned referee.

Having played for Anderlecht I am often asked how European clubs would perform in top flight English football. As a player, I felt that only the likes of Ajax, Bayern Munich, AC Milan and Feyenoord at their pomp would have been successful. In the modern era I doubt whether clubs such as Real Madrid, Barcelona or either of the Milan teams would win the Premier League although winning the FA Cup or League Cup is always a possibility. You have to face facts that the best players are predominantly in England and it's set to stay that way.

Football salaries have always been hot gossip as far back as I remember and top players will continue to demand top dollar wages. Salaries increased at a pace in my day but most players still relied on a testimonial match to kick-start a retirement fund if they were fortunate. In my case, I was not at a club long enough to receive a bonus game but I played in plenty of them. Also, we could not retire when we hung up our boots, unlike modern day top stars who can retire if they wish to. Nowadays, top stars don't need a testimonial. One long term Premier League contract earning in a week what most ordinary punters only dream of in a year means they are made for life. You cannot blame a player for taking the best contract available. Anyone would do so in their position but credit to the likes of a number of players who arranged a testimonial to benefit charities. Maybe that is the way ahead for the superstars to give something back. Whenever salaries are discussed, agents' roles are not far behind. Agents play a key role and have changed the face of football forever. Although they are looking after clients' interests it does not surprise me when supporters say the sport has lost its soul, and they are not wrong in my view. Inflated wages for substandard players is bad enough, but when that results in fans paying extortionate ticket prices to watch a game so clubs can recoup huge outlays, you cannot blame supporters for demanding success instantly, as they are spending hard-earned money. Salaries, agents and ticket prices are all laterally linked whatever football clubs pay. Fans pay their money so they have a right to an opinion especially when some players appear to go through the motions.

Hooliganism is another hot potato that rears itself from time to time and never quite seems to go away. It afflicted the mid-seventies to late-eighties and during my career I experienced many hairy moments. Witnessing supporters caged into stadiums was not a pleasant sight. It was so different from my early years in the game when supporters packed the terraces with no segregation. Travelling to and from matches has had its scary moments. On more than one occasion lads had to take evasive action following an away victory as bricks smashed through the team coach windows. I fully understand fans being passionate but I have always been amazed at the psyche of a lunatic fringe that have no angst in causing criminal damage, maiming players or opposing fans. It took a major disaster for the football world to take a long hard look at itself. No one living in Liverpool will ever forget the shockwaves caused by the Hillsborough disaster in 1989. All-seater stadia have helped but, worryingly, tensions are still prevalent. Thankfully, the worst of the bad old days of football hooliganism seems to have disappeared. But in isolated incidents globally, there are still occurrences where supporters have even been killed, which is crazy. I know football is tribal but other high profile sports never get such extreme reactions that bring shame on the sport. Arguably stakes are higher financially but it's still only a football match not a war.

Technology is another popular conversation point. I would not change the rules of the game radically as they have stood the test of time. I think that technology must be brought into the game as the financial stakes are so high nowadays: relegation can affect the very existence of a club and one good or bad decision might decide an important title. Officials in present day matches can now communicate as they are wired up to each other and that is good for the game, but there could be a fifth official constantly watching a monitor from different angles. I realise that it may not be practical to have numerous monitors available at all grounds but grounds could at least use goal line technology. I have lost count of the number of times a referee has awarded a goal, or not as the case may be, in important games or made bad decisions at crucial moments. You only have to look back at the Champions League semi-final when Liverpool overcame Chelsea with a very dubious goal to illustrate the point. And last season Chelsea were on the receiving end of some dodgy decisions at the same stage against Barcelona. You could not get more high profile games. Sadly there are countless examples of this happening every season. I realise football is not a play-by-play sport like rugby league, tennis or cricket, but other sports where technology helps should be analysed. In rugby league, when a try is scored and a referee is not sure then the try is viewed to get the correct call. And it's the same with cricket, although a lot easier because play is stopped after every ball. In football, when the ball is out of play there is time to reflect. Football fans are knowledgeable and if a rule came in for a fifth official to make a call, I'm sure supporters would buy into it. A referee could still have an overriding call if he felt the incident was not in the spirit of the game although he could be made to explain his thinking.

Talking of refs and the recent respect campaign in England,

one simple rule that would solve many issues is to take a leaf out of both rugby codes concerning dissent. If a player shows dissent to a decision, then penalise the relevant team 10 yards and if it goes all the way back to a penalty, then so be it. That one ruling, however harsh it seems, would stop dissent. Why should footballers be able to harass a referee to the point of assaulting him? It does not happen in other sports and football should be no different. Dissent sends a dreadful message to wannabee fans watching. It's not difficult to realise why many replicate it on playing fields the next day in amateur football where referees have no support. The cycle permeates through grassroots football and does untold damage. When I see some of the players' antics on the field I am not surprised the refereeing authorities struggle to recruit new officials.

These areas of debate, and more, make Question and Answer Sessions at times riveting from both sides of the fence at dinners, and I enjoy taking part in them immensely. A regular feature of my stand-up routine, which I also particularly enjoy, is recalling some of my sporting heroes outside football. I love watching other sports, particularly cricket, which stems from my years at Nottingham Forest when I was able to witness the great Sir Garfield Sobers play. An early boyhood hero was South Africa-born cricketer Basil D'Oliveira who, because of apartheid, played for Worcestershire and England. Many people applauded D'Oliveira for his stance, along with top England players and he was a fine cricketer. Another South African to make a mark in recent years is Kevin Pietersen. KP is world class and has had the same impact as Andrew 'Freddie' Flintoff in the 2005 Ashes. Confidence is key in any sport and when they are on fire then entertainers feel that they can do anything. KP is an entertainer at the highest level and has confidence in abundance. He is a true crowd pleaser.

In my day, Ian Botham (known as 'Both') was the equivalent to both KP and Flintoff. 'Both' was a breath of fresh air and lit up the Ashes series in 1981. He used to make me laugh. I remember him saying that the only thing that frightened him was sitting in a car with Brian Close driving, not his bowling or batting! On and off the park, 'Both' was a larger than life character. In many ways, he was a guy out of a comic book strip, a real super hero. Being an all-rounder, Ian had twice the chance to be the hero but this carried twice the pressure. A batsman can always get a duck batting and then be out of the game, but that never applied to 'Both' as he could go out and redeem himself by getting five wickets. When he took the new ball or walked to the crease there was an air of anticipation, and more often than not this giant of a cricketer delivered big time whether he was a batsman or bowler. 'Both' could carry the weight of expectation like few other players preceding his career or since.

Of all the flamboyant cricketers I've seen down the years, and there have been plenty, such as Clive Lloyd, Vivian Richards, Sachin Tendulkar, Imran Khan and Shane Warne, in my view none of them can touch Garfield Sobers. If ever there was a one-man team then Sobers was it. And as luck would have it, I have become good friends with him on the after-dinner circuit during the summer months. Gary lives North of Bridgetown on a beautiful strip of the West Coast of Barbados but comes over to England for a couple of months every year, partly due to his position as Minister of Tourism, but also to join the circuit during the cricket season. He is always a great draw. It's a tremendous bonus when I'm at the same event and there is a buzz of anticipation when he speaks.

Back to the modern era and twenty20 cricket is all the rage nowadays. It really is an exciting format of the sport. It's what fans want and you have to move with the times but there is still room for Test cricket for the connoisseur. The county game has been stagnant for years and it amazes me that we still have this format as it is played midweek when there are only a few hundred hardy souls watching. How on earth can they inspire performances? Sports people thrive on atmosphere and county cricket fails to deliver. Fans deserve better. In the twenty20 format, crowds pack stadia and think 'Wow this is terrific entertainment'. There is no doubt that twenty20 cricket is here to stay.

All my heroes seem to be great characters so it's no surprise that Lee Trevino was a player who appealed to me from the world of golf, though there are more accomplished players in the likes of Jack Nicklaus, Seve Ballesteros and more recently Tiger Woods. Seve is the closest to Trevino in terms of entertaining but there was something about Trevino in the golden era aside Nicklaus, Tom Watson and Arnold Palmer that made him special. Trevino did things that little bit differently and entertained when the pressure was at its height. He was also talkative during a round, but I'm not so sure his playing partners were quite as enamoured as the massive crowds that lined the course. Trevino, like Bestie and Botham in their pomp, was fabulous for the golfing game.

Another legendary sporting character for me is Ilie Nastase who wowed tennis crowds in the late sixties and early seventies. I saw Nastase play when the tour came to Nottingham prior to Wimbledon and he was audacious in his stroke play. Nastase is an entertainer in every sense of the word. When it was raining Nastase would walk on with his umbrella, all set to play, and the crowd lapped it up. I have always admired entertainers, which is why I was also a big John McEnroe fan, despite his tantrums. I did wonder whether some of it was stage-managed but mostly it seemed for real. McEnroe, of course, has gone on to become the best tennis summariser on television. He is in huge demand and it is always a joy to hear him during his analysis of a top match.

In recent times, Johnny Wilkinson and Martin Johnson turned people on to rugby union when they led England to the World Cup a few years ago and I've also been a keen follower of horse racing. Lester Piggott was the star when I grew up but in the modern era there is no one more famous or flamboyant than Frankie Dettori, who became a sporting icon when he rode all seven winners at Ascot. Frankie is a top entertainer whether he's in the saddle or playing golf as I've discovered at charity events. Frankie, on one memorable occasion, shaved a hole and theatrically rolled over. Of course, the watching public loved every bit of his showmanship and it was so easy to see why.

Pro-am golf tournaments are fantastic to take part in and I'm lucky enough to have been invited to many for deserving charities. They can be anywhere from Jakarta to La Manga to Turnberry. Events attract ex-pros such as Kenny Dalglish and Alan Hansen together with the likes of Rick Wakeman, Nigel Mansell, Jimmy Tarbuck, Sean Connery and Bruce Forsyth. There were many celebrities but for me the tops was to play in the same round as Sir Norman Wisdom, God bless him. Norman now lives in a retirement home but he's still entertaining and, hopefully, the old magic will never desert him. On the golf course, Norman was always a scream and kept putting players off shots but it was all for a good cause. And of course, it did not take long for him to pull a famous pose with his flat cap and sing the odd tune. Norman really is an amazing character and played in charity golf tournaments for years. As he approached his nineties, he'd play three holes if the weather were fine or one hole if it was inclement before heading off to the clubhouse. And then there is Tarby who is a great character and football daft. Of course, being a devoted Liverpool fan, there is always plenty of banter when we meet and he is always popular with crowds.

After-dinner speaking has moved on apace for me, which has been fantastic. Working the smaller gigs was important and I still enjoy entertaining at such venues but as my confidence, ability and maturity developed, I progressed further up the corporate ladder. Often I go to a venue and pinch myself that 25 years after finishing playing, people are thirsty for gags from my era as a player. In recent years, I have been privileged to entertain on cruise liners. Of course, you have a captive audience because they can't go far (although there is other entertainment on board) but it is terrific fun.

Despite all my experience, I was particularly nervous for an address at the Duke of Edinburgh awards at Windsor Castle in front of Prince Edward and leading sports personalities. Entertaining Royalty along with sporting icons from the world of football, cricket and rugby union and Olympic champions was unnerving but I soon settled down and it was a real hoot to see Prince Edward laughing. Meeting him afterwards, I found Prince Edward very pleasant, but my favourite Royal is Princess Anne, who is always approachable, natural and makes me feel at ease.

Doing a gig like the Duke of Edinburgh awards is hugely rewarding in terms of prestige but it's not just because of the Royal touch. What made the event particularly special for me was when Olympic ice dance champion Christopher Dean, from Torvill and Dean, made a point of coming over to say he really enjoyed watching me during my Nottingham Forest days when he was a kid. I thought to myself, 'He's an Olympic gold medallist and I never won any major honour yet he appreciated my career.' It's very humbling and means an awful lot to a former footballer who had dreams of making it big when growing up in Grimsby.

I have a wonderful second career because I bump into players I've not seen for years as well as many a sporting celebrity. There is tremendous camaraderie between the old lads at Everton with Dave Hickson, Graham Sharp, Jim Pearson and Alan Whittle, and celebrity guests such as jockey Martin Dwyer, high jumper Steve Smith and snooker ace John Parrott. All are big Evertonians and it's great seeing them. And it's the same at Leeds United with Paul Reaney, Norman Hunter, Mick Jones, Allan Clarke and occasionally Frank Worthington. The crack is always fantastic. People love to hear gags about Cloughie, my time at Leeds United and Everton as well as the greats from the seventies, for which I am eternally thankful.

12

THE MODERN ERA

The Premier League is the most competitive in the world. Because of the mega money on offer, top foreign players are attracted. In the late seventies, football was on a different platform, as very few stars from Europe played in England. British teams competed in Europe at the highest level and set the standards, especially in the European Cup. Ajax, Bayern Munich and Liverpool dominated, while Nottingham Forest also made a mark. In the modern era, the Champions League brings together top teams and English clubs regularly get to the latter stages. Three teams made the 2007–08 semi-finals while the final featured the top two in England, Manchester United and Chelsea. And last season again three English teams made the last four before Barcelona stunned Manchester United to claim the top European prize. England has not won a global prize for over 40 years, yet the best players in Europe are based in England and have made the Premier League the top division to watch around the world. Viewing figures are staggering and it's no wonder all the top English teams have to make pre-and post-season tours to distant countries. The trend is set to continue and it's only a matter of time before the so-called 39th game is introduced.

Sadly, the modern day player is detached. Top stars are multi-millionaires. They can purchase the best car money can buy and the most luxurious homes. They don't stay in five-star hotels because they expect 'exclusive' hotels. The likes of Rooney, Ronaldo and co. can buy anything they desire from a young age and live in a different world to the majority of people. Premier League stars are totally remote from even the 'prawn sandwich' brigade who pay top prices to watch them play. Remuneration for footballers has moved on to almost Hollywood status. But the majority of players from my day don't resent the wages current players command because they would have jumped at earning as much given the chance. We earned good money but nothing close to the scale of modern day footballers. Sky investment dictates, and massive wages are the result, so players quite rightly get a slice of the action because they are serving up the entertainment. I don't blame the top players but it is out of shape with reality.

With the trappings of wealth, though, there is a downside when things go wrong. Players are taken from a comfortable environment and put in a place they cannot handle. Pressures are immense while they are playing and when it's all over, a number struggle to adapt to life away from the game. Apart from Bestie, no one in my day had 24/7 media attention. Current top stars and managers see every aspect of life reported 24/7 if it will offer up a story. And the media frenzy for scoops has had its casualties. The modern-day Bestie in terms of media attention is Paul Gascoigne and do I feel for Gazza! I am thankful I never experienced anything like the intrusive media he has had.

Spiralling wages for elite footballers have alienated supporters and that is the saddest aspect of the modern game. Without harping on about the past, supporters could approach us before games, after games, during the week in the street or at a restaurant, and we'd happily sign autographs. We also knew that it was important to attend supporters' club events. It was not part of our job description, but it was an unwritten rule of what we were expected to do and there was terrific banter. Our lifestyle was very different to the modern day footballer. There was a different relationship at the top level between players and fans. It's not so much that current players won't sign autographs, many have come from humble backgrounds and understand a player-fan philosophy, but the powers that be at top clubs won't allow fans access to star players. I feel for today's fans because the older generation of supporters have been brought up with a totally different philosophy. Top clubs have created something of a mystique about their star turns who often hide away in security-clad mansions.

Clubs were seen as very much a part of the community, but in the main that has disappeared at the top level. Players train under immense security behind closed doors and press conferences are stage-managed. When I played, fans watched us train without issues. Those days though are gone forever. Mega money will damage the game because true supporters will tire of being sidelined and taken for a ride with rising ticket and replica shirt prices. The working man in the street who was the traditional lifeblood for clubs simply cannot afford inflated ticket prices and many are resentful of so-called stars who in reality are no more than ordinary players.

The days of sell-out crowds up and down the country appear to be on the slide. Premier League clubs last season like Bolton Wanderers, Blackburn, Middlesbrough, West Ham and Sunderland struggled to attract a full house when the big clubs came to play, and this is sending out a dangerous message. Also there is no competition at the highest level apart from among the big four. Breaking into the quartet of Chelsea, Manchester United, Liverpool and Arsenal appears out of reach unless a few more Russian billionaires turn up. The big four are getting stronger and other clubs are scrapping away just to get into Europe or survive. It is a massive gap, though Aston Villa and

Everton have made an impact recently. For all the problems, I don't think foreign players should be limited.

Television coverage has also gone through the roof. From the time of *Match of the Day* on a Saturday night covering two or three games then the equivalent around the regions on ITV the following day, no league games were covered live apart from the FA Cup final. Even the League Cup final was just highlights and England games failed to get live coverage apart from the clash with Scotland in the Home Internationals. Football fans born in the last 20 years would think we came from another planet. There is so much football on television nowadays that fans can take or leave it. As for image rights, they were not even on the radar in my day but now it's common place. The endorsements available to players are unbelievable. Football has come a long way from advertising Brylcreem in the fifties. Nowadays you name it and it's advertised.

Despite all the current issues discussed earlier, overall I think that the modern game is superior in some respects. When I played, players and spectators had common values. Now they never meet. They are on a different plain altogether. But there is no denying the spectacle of a football match is better televised. There are also better stadia, pitches, marketing and the surroundings to it all. Football is a truly global game. Any other topic in the world that has been so saturated in the media would have been dead and buried by now. People would have been sick of it but the stories keep coming and none more so in recent times than those surrounding David Beckham.

Becks is a very shrewd lad and has never been anything else throughout his career. He knows exactly how to market his fame and Brand Beckham would not have got to the level that it has achieved without David having a sensible head on his shoulders. Football ability and good looks alone do not guarantee the degree of success he's had in England, Spain, the United States and most recently Italy. Marketing is essential but Beckham knows that he must be able to deliver on the pitch and there is nobody with a sweeter right foot than him when it comes to set pieces. Without doubt David is the player of his generation. When Beckham joined Real Madrid, his new superstar teammates could not believe the entourage that accompanied him. But it was not long before Zidane, Ronaldo, Figo and Roberto Carlos were won over by this extraordinary individual both as a person and footballer. They could only marvel at his marketability because Beckham is truly a global star. To his credit, football has always been the main issue for David and when Fabio Capello dropped him from the side, Beckham won his place back by delivering the right attitude in training even though it was announced he was leaving for the States. It was no surprise to me that he forced his way back into the England squad. This is because Capello knows Beckham inspires others when training and on the pitch. When Becks takes the field, there is a reaction on and off the park.

As for Wayne Rooney, he doesn't crave the media attention and is a totally different character. All Wayne wants to do is play football. Rooney lives for the game and it's wonderful to see because when he is on song there isn't a more dangerous player in the game. Wayne does not court publicity; he just wants to get on with his football. I watched him grow up as an apprentice at Everton and he was some talent. Rooney is a great kid, a fantastic footballer and has the game to dominate at the highest level for the next decade at least, if he stays injury free. Wayne has the drive and potential to win a record number of England caps and score the most goals for his country so long as he is not played out of position. Rooney sees everything around him and his vision on the pitch is incredible. Wayne always knows where players are. I'd give him a free role. Sir Alex knew what he was doing when he signed

Rooney. When they played together for Manchester United, Ronaldo saw Rooney on occasion, Rooney saw Ronaldo all the time. Wayne Rooney is a world class player. With Ronaldo moving on to Real Madrid for his world record £80 million fee, Rooney will have more responsibility at United but he'll still deliver.

Regarding managers, my old team mate Martin O'Neill really impresses me. As a player Martin did not have the greatest confidence in his ability, which was crazy because he had it in abundance. He was a very good player. As a young kid trying to make his way in the game, Martin was studious and careful about what he said. Nothing has changed. Since becoming a manager, Martin has a fabulous ability to give players a chance to shine. When he took over from David O'Leary at Aston Villa, Martin didn't shun any players. He brought players in and made them feel a part of the club. It's no surprise that he is making a success of his post at Villa. The club have made steady progress year on year and that is down to Martin, backed by a chairman allowing him time and space to deliver the goods. Martin has a knack of making players feel a million dollars. He also has an uncanny ability to marry up players to what is required on the park. Loyalty is essential. You always see his players stand by him and he gets results. Martin has the utmost belief in his ability. During a summer of madness, only Martin managed to hang on to a star asset when Liverpool came calling for Gareth Barry. Credit to Martin for sticking to his guns. Getting Barry to stay last season was a minor miracle. Very few managers could have achieved that result. Martin will succeed both at Villa and with any future posts he takes up, just as he did at Leicester City and Celtic.

Mark Hughes is another manager I rate highly. Currently presiding at Manchester City, Mark has a war chest available that managers can only dream about. With the investment he now has at his fingertips, Mark has an opportunity to make a mark at the highest level. But there is enormous pressure on him to deliver. I believe, given time, he is up to the challenge. Having the opportunity to buy any player is no easy task but Mark could well be the man to bring back success to City. He is quiet, knowledgeable, yet steely. They always say beware the quiet man and Mark is such a person. Never be worried about the player who says he'll do this and that, and it's the same with a manager. In the dressing room, Mark makes his presence felt. Mark has worked under Sir Alex Ferguson and Terry Venables. That type of experience is invaluable and I'm sure he will prove to be a great success.

As for Roy Keane, who got Sunderland promoted before resigning, he's worked under the best two managers this country has produced in Brian Clough (when he started out as a teenager at Nottingham Forest) and Sir Alex (when he made his name at Manchester United). Roy has the temperament of Ray Wilkins (who is knowledgeable but too nice to be a manager) but allies it with the mean streak of Cloughie. Don't be fooled by this relaxed approach, Roy kicks every ball and will not hesitate in letting a player know what he thinks in the dressing room. Having seen and done it as a player, Roy gains immediate respect from players. His achievements at Sunderland, when no one gave them a prayer of surviving in the Premier League, speak volumes about his ability. Only time will tell if he makes it but I'm confident we have not seen the last of this great warrior.

Sam Allardyce is a real character and the game needs managers like him. At Bolton Wanderers, Sam over-achieved and I was surprised how long he was on the sidelines following his tenure at Newcastle United before taking over from Paul Ince at Blackburn Rovers. Sam will steady the ship and take my former club forward. His exit on Tyneside was ridiculous because he was given no time to develop a team, but Kevin Keegan's return was always on the cards. In Newcastle, Kevin is the Messiah. His initial spell as boss was a case of so near yet so far, but they produced some magical football such as the day they knocked in five against Manchester United. Albert's chip to make it five was the icing on the cake and sent St James' Park into raptures. Newcastle has among the most fervent supporters in the game and King Kev could do no wrong. Losing the title was heartbreaking because Newcastle's style of play was so exciting and they deserved to win the league, but Kevin lost it towards the end as Sir Alex won through mind games. His departure from Newcastle was just as farcical as Big Sam's. Alan Shearer stepped in but could not save his beloved Newcastle from relegation. Newcastle followers are fantastic but it's a poisoned chalice in many ways for any boss trying to bring back the glory days.

Managers in the modern era are so different from the guys at the helm in the mid-seventies and trying to explain the old managers' attributes to young kids nowadays is nigh on impossible. Top managers are well remunerated but are now in a situation where they have to work with a squad of multi-millionaires and appeal to their professional pride. We were just grateful to be in the game and earning a living for something we loved doing. It's no good for a Premiership manager to go into a changing room screaming and shouting because there is a different mentality and philosophy. Even the likes of Cloughie and Shanks would think they were on a different planet in the modern game as they have to deal with agents and the way football is geared to the corporate world.

In the current economic climate, top clubs and others down the footballing pyramid will undoubtedly follow the demise of my former club Leeds United. Watching Leeds go from Champions League semi-finalists to the third tier of English football was heartbreaking, but chasing the dream proved to be a nightmare. Financial prudency has to be the way forward for all clubs. Many clubs are trying to compete with the mega money teams including another of my former clubs, Everton, who ran into problems pre-Rooney. When Rooney left for Manchester United for a big fee it was a case of 'Thank God for that', as it got Everton out of a massive financial hole and you can understand why the board took the decision. It upset Evertonians at the time but it was the right decision in the long term. Look across Stanley Park to the Liverpool owners who say they are fully committed but the long-term implications of the credit crunch will test their resolve. The money that has to be generated just to pay the interest before a player kicks a ball is mind-blowing.

Financially, outside the top two of Manchester United and Chelsea (recently Manchester City have also fallen into that bracket following the Dubai-based takeover), competing at the highest level is nigh on impossible despite the incredible talent pool of players at Liverpool and Arsenal. And supporters are going to have to get used to it. Long gone are the days when a number of teams can compete in England for major trophies. But the English game has been fortunate because they were one of the few countries where that applied in Europe during the early seventies. Having two or three clubs dominating the game domestically has been around for forever and a day elsewhere. What is happening in England is what has been the case in Europe for years when only a few teams compete. It's a far cry from my era when there were more winners. A team could come from nowhere and triumph, but times move on.

In Scotland only two clubs have dominated the scene for years. Aberdeen had a brief period of dominance and Hearts challenged briefly but Celtic versus Rangers is the only game in town. In Belgium it was Anderlecht and Bruges, and before that it was Standard Liege and Antwerp. In Spain, it's the two Madrid sides, Barcelona and at a pinch Valencia. In Germany, Bayern

Munich were the dominant force in my day and nothing has changed. France has never been a major footballing country when it comes to club football. There were doubts in 1998, when they hosted the World Cup, about filling the stadia because there was a feeling the French were not interested in the sport sufficiently as the Tour de France was their big event. As it transpired French stars returned home and they were victorious. The crowds were massive but club football has not grown. All the best players play in more competitive leagues.

Supporters may not like seeing a few clubs dominate but just as players have to get on with it, although it's a no-brainer as they are well remunerated, so have supporters. They will have to get used to the fact that their team is playing for scraps and the occasional trophy when they can spring a surprise. As for teams in the lower echelons such as my hometown club of Grimsby Town, they can only expect to produce a couple of kids, get a sizeable fee and move up to the next level but it's a slow process.

The fear factor in the modern game is by far the biggest problem. There is so much pressure due to the media bandwagon on a daily and match basis. Managers lose jobs far too early in a season, as there is that constant worry that comes from relegation, which could set a club back years. Yo-yo clubs like Sunderland, and West Brom in recent years, have benefited by having something to play for in terms of relegation or promotion, but in the main clubs that get promotion don't spend a fortune any more. Those days are gone. Look at Reading, Watford and Derby. All three teams were promoted and then relegated before fans could settle into the top league. Prudently they decided not to invest heavily in mad salaries on players, but it's a hard balancing act. The old argument of spending to survive does not hold. Promoted clubs must not spend beyond their means. It's tough to go down and come back in a bid to manage the transition sensibly but that may be the only way forward. Avoiding a boom and bust situation has to be the way ahead. Just ask Leeds fans who are suffering following double relegation because the club lived the dream a few years back. Unless a billionaire comes in, it will take years for them to get back to Champions League status as all the best players get snapped up. Just look at the quality academy players who have moved on in recent years such as Kewell, Harte, Smith, Robinson, Woodgate, Carson, Lennon and Milner, with Delph next on the list.

Sadly, the Premier League has become the billionaires' playground. The Manchester City deal is amazing and has stuck two fingers up at Manchester United and Liverpool. These major deals are not great for the game because it is just turning it into a circus. For me the Curbishley and Keegan departures last season summed up all that is wrong with the modern game. King Kev does wear his heart on his sleeve but he had a point when he departed for a second time. A manager has to have the overriding say over whom he wishes to purchase. You cannot have a situation where the moneymen dictate everything, but Champions League football is critical. Without it you cannot attract the top players and unless you have a chairman or consortium that will fund you, then as a club it spells danger. Failure is potentially catastrophic. The game has moved into a different global sphere and for me it is a worry that billionaires will soon own all the top clubs.

Football finances dictate and put history aside. On Merseyside I can sadly see the day when Liverpool and Everton will ground share. There is great banter between the two clubs but there is vitriol among fans on this topic who have worshipped heroes at Anfield and Goodison. However, the sensible option is a joint stadium. Whether the two sets of fans would vote for this is doubtful with all the history involved, but it has worked in

Milan where there is intense rivalry. When push comes to shove, though, shareholders will decide and economies of scale will take precedent. One fact is inescapable; both clubs need bigger stadia to generate bigger capacities and more income. There is an emotional road to travel first, though.

Finances across football have got bigger. What I hope is that as more money comes into the game we get a balance. It would be bad if all the money went on wages. Some must go to enhance the sport at grassroots level, as that is how to produce stars of the future and encourage more people to play the game. Currently we are in danger of the Premier League breaking away and alienating true football supporters. More and more fans say things like 'I can't afford to follow my team as prices for away supporters are extortionate.' Something has to give for the future of the game. I can see the day coming sooner rather than later when the Premier League becomes two divisions of 12 teams with the top tier playing European football. Finances are everything at this level but sadly there will be casualties as the moneymen come and go. Fans will remain to pick up the pieces.

It's a worrying time for followers of the sport, though die-hard supporters will not abandon the club, however I suspect many of the younger generation will follow one of the big guns. The days of footballing family dynasties are dead. With the advent of the Internet and Sky, kids from small towns cotton on to successful clubs. Just walk down a high street in any city, you will see a range of replica shirts and they won't only be the local club unless you're in London, Manchester or Glasgow. In the lower leagues of professional football without Sky money, clubs have to live within their means. While they don't compete at a high level, sensible pricing of tickets at some clubs has brought fans back who are priced out of the market at the Premier League clubs. Maybe that is the only positive to come out of madcap finances.

13

IT'S BEEN FUN FOR THE KID FROM GRIMSBY

I've been dealt a great hand since my heyday as a footballer because I've been pretty successful on the after-dinner circuit and in other media outlets. Opportunities to move into these industries were both unexpected surprises when they first came about because my career was only just in full swing at Everton. I've always got on with supporters and was happy to be in the midst of journalists. The fact that I was also blessed with an ability to chat away meant that these niches were a natural future direction for me.

Giving views on referees, new technology, the professional foul, salaries, football agents, club versus country, foreign imports and so on is second nature to me and I'm delighted to express my views with more than a few anecdotal stories thrown in for good measure. I'm happy with the road I've travelled. My speeches followa set pattern in some respects, but they have evolved and depend very much on the audience. I always mix past with present. I've been fortunate to be well received and people seem to like my sense of humour. It's crazy when I look back because I didn't consciously try to break into the worlds of speaking engagements, radio, TV or journalism, they all just came my way. And I'm very thankful because it's given me a second career in the sport that I fell in love with when growing up in Grimsby.

Lots of players from the sixties and seventies are bitter with how life has treated them since hanging up their boots. This is sad, but we played in an era when there was little advice on planning for the future. I understand their frustration because when they see ordinary players become multi-millionaires who will never have to work again, it does rankle some lads. All I can say is that my life has been great and I'm a lucky lad because I have a great family, a wonderful job and material items have never interested me. Family life has always been the stability I've needed. Dot has been the rock in my life and long may our partnership continue. Our son, Andrew, became a professional golfer, played on the South African tour and a few European tour events but quickly realised the standards you have to reach year on year. He now runs his own golf events company. Our daughter Riah recently graduated with a Science degree and is working in the pharmaceuticals industry.

I look back at my playing era with pride because it was a terrific time to play football. I'm constantly asked to compare generations of footballers but I refuse to do this. I would never turn around to a youngster and say the late sixties and seventies were better because every team had star players, there was more competition at the top and trophies were shared around. That would be wrong. You can only play in the era you're born and make the best of it. Having said that, I do believe the swinging sixties were a great time to grow up in because of the music and kids being able to play in the streets safely. This era has disappeared forever but being a footballer, you have to aim for the top in the time that you play. The cream will always rise to the top and while wages are amazing, fewer young guns in England get them because of foreign imports, so it's tough to make it. For those that do, I wish them good look and I'm delighted to be able to discuss them on the circuit.

As a professional footballer, John Toshack used to say that I was akin to a Rolls Royce that spent most of its career in the garage. Thanks John, but I suppose in many ways that just about summed me up. My form got me into the England set-up, though a full cap eluded me. But nobody could say I was not good enough to play for England because I was there or thereabouts on the fringes. Many pundits said I didn't work hard enough to play for England, but that did not stop Shanks telling me he should have come in for me when he signed Kevin Keegan from Scunthorpe United. Tosh may quip that Shanks spun that yarn to many a footballer, but just being praised by the great man was sufficient acclaim to my abilities.

Making it at the highest level in football is often about being in the right place at the right time and of course you cannot help but wonder what would have happened if I'd played for someone like Shanks at that particular time. Life is not about ifs, buts and maybes. You can't have regrets otherwise they just swallow you up. I played for some cracking teams and entertained supporters around the country. What more can you want from a career?

Whenever I meet football fans around the country, someone always says, 'Duncan you were one of my favourite players', and that is a terrific feeling. To me there are good players and eye-catching good players. I'd like to think that I was an eye-catching good player. Rev Harry Ross officiates at the church at Goodison Park. I was chatting to him one day and told him I felt a tad embarrassed because I only played at Goodison for 10 minutes compared to some of the other lads who played 500 plus games, yet I was included in the Everton Hall of Fame. Rev Harry turned around and said, 'Duncan it's what you did in the 10 minutes that counts.' It's hard to analyse a career when you are going through it, but 25 years on from my heyday, it's conversations like that which make me appreciate my career all the more.

Being dubbed a Fancy Dan stayed with me throughout my career, but how could I have any regrets about being known as an entertainer or a so-called maverick when judged alongside the likes of Bowles, Worthington, Marsh and Currie? It's an honour and privilege to be in such company and we followed the greatest entertainer of the swinging sixties, Georgie Best. Fans either acknowledged my skills or bemoaned my reputation as a luxury in a team. My approach to football was one I have no regrets about and I have lost count of the number of times fans of all clubs have recalled a game when they wished I were in their side. Football supporters want excitement and memorable moments of magic. I tried to deliver just that.

Followers of football always look back nostalgically. I was not successful in terms of winning medals and caps, but just as there were great goal scorers, dynamic schemers, hatchet defenders and flamboyant keepers, so everyone knows of the entertainers and I was proud to be one. Managers did not truly appreciate the likes of me along with Stan, Frank, Rodney and Tony but football supporters loved a crowd-pleaser going back to the times of Matthews and Best. We may not have been in their exalted class but in the mid-seventies we provided true entertainment in an era of mainly method football. We had an unofficial Ball Players Union and stuck up for each other. There is a danger of looking back with rose-tinted spectacles but these lads could play. I often joke at dinners that I was a good player when I played, a great player when I finished and a legend now. Long may it reign!

If there was misfortune to my career then maybe I didn't play under the right manager at the right time. When Cloughie took over at Nottingham Forest in 1975, he wanted to sign me, but Leeds would not do business and then when he came in for me at Everton, they would also not do business. I'm convinced I'd have flourished under Cloughie given the chance, but it was not to be. Saying that, playing for Cloughie might also have made my career go pear-shaped. Returning to a former club rarely works but it's all conjecture as my career took a different route.

On the park, I always tried to entertain because that was my style. Football supporters often ask me whether I think the modern game is more entertaining and when I think of the likes of Ronaldo with his dribbling skills, it's tough to argue that the old game was more entertaining. But then again, I just point out the hatchet men we had to avoid and pitches we played on. The discussion then grinds to a halt! In my view, there are various ways of looking at entertainment. We had the entertainment, or challenge, of playing on appalling surfaces where the grass was threadbare to say the least. The ball would bobble on an uneven surface and mistakes could occur. Players could easily slip-slide around and bear in mind that during my era, a referee only called a game off when the ground was deemed unsafe for the spectators. Matches were rarely called off because it was unsafe for the players. If terraces were safe, then snow on the pitch was shovelled to the sidelines. Many grounds did not have the benefit of undersoil heating so surfaces could be rock hard. Today, top players have the advantage of playing on pitches like a billiard table. I'd love to have had such a luxury week in and week out. On top of poor surfaces, we also had to combat a defender trying to maim us. I'd pay good money to see Ronaldo taking on 'Bites Yer Legs' Hunter or 'Chopper' Harris at the old Baseball Ground!

Players complain about tackles from behind, in fact they complain about almost any type of tackle. Never was a sixth sense more necessary in my heyday and I was fortunate. As a player I always felt that I had two great assets. I was blessed with a good first touch but, just as important, I was also blessed with a sixth sense for where problems were coming from. It was not just the cloggers looking to take me out, but I could feel my way out of a dangerous situation. A good first touch always makes a ball player look a class act. Instant control was a key factor for me.

I always moaned when teammates in defence failed to pass when I was unmarked. My argument was that just booting the ball over the back four for me to chase was a fruitless exercise. It was not my game. Punting the ball gave them a 30-second to a minute rest bite before the ball came back, whereas passing it gave me a 50–50 chance of making something of the possession. Football, in my view, was about confidence in making something happen. I had bags of confidence and wanted to take the opportunity to prove it. I always tried to entertain. That was my game and the way I played. You have to be realistic about who and what you are and what you are best at doing.

Pundits and supporters have often said I should have played for England. The opportunity to play for England just once would have been fantastic, but it was not to be and that has always been my philosophy. The crazy thing is that I see people who genuinely think I played for England. Compères still introduce me as Duncan McKenzie of Everton, Leeds United and England. I've given up correcting them! There were one or two hard luck stories when I felt aggrieved, such as not playing in the European and League Cup final when it really mattered. Mostly I have no regrets. I played against all the great players from a wonderful era of football and I still see many of them around the country. I travel all over and am immensely surprised still to be involved in the game. It's a humble feeling, a quarter of a century after I finished playing, that people still want to hear about my experiences. For a young kid kicking the ball about on the streets of Grimsby, I've come a long way and it's been a blast.

DUNCAN McKENZIE PLAYING CAREER

FOOTBALL LEAGUE	Season	Division	League		FA Cup		League Cup		Europe/Ch Shld		Total Apps.	Total Goals
			Apps.	Goals	Apps.	Goals	Apps.	Goals	Apps.	Goals		
Nottingham Forest	1969-70	1	1	0							1	0
Mansfield Town (loan)	1969-70	3	10	3							10	3
Nottingham Forest	1970-71	1	5 (3)	2			0 (1)				5 (4)	2
Nottingham Forest	1971-72	1	31 (2)	7			3	3			34 (2)	10
Nottingham Forest	1972-73	2	27 (1)	6			1	0			28 (1)	6
Mansfield Town (loan)	1972-73	4	6	7							6	7
Nottingham Forest	1973-74	2	41	26	6	2	2	0			49	28
Leeds United	1974-75	1	26 (1)	11	4 (3)	2	3	0	1 (1)	0	34 (5)	13
Leeds United	1975-76	1	38 (1)	16	2	0	2	1			42 (1)	17
Everton	1976-77	1	20	5	6	4	4	1			30	10
Everton	1977-78	1	28	9	1 (1)	1	2	1			31 (1)	11
Chelsea	1978-79	1	15	4	1	0					16	4
Blackburn Rovers	1978-79	2	13	2							13	2
Blackburn Rovers	1979-80	3	42	12	7	1	4	3			53	16
Blackburn Rovers	1980-81	2	19	2	1	0	4	1			24	3
TOTALS											**376 (14)**	**132**

BELGIUM LEAGUE			Apps.	Goals							Total Apps.	Total Goals
Anderlecht	1976-77	1	30	16							30	16

NASL*			Apps.	Goals							Total Apps.	Total Goals
Tulsa Roughnecks	1981	Central	33	14							33	14
Chicago Sting	1982	Eastern	20	3							20	3
CAREER TOTALS											**459 (14)**	**165**

Duncan also played for Royden, Hong Kong in 1983   *NASL: National American Soccer League